40 DAYS

Prayers and Devotions to Prepare for the Second Coming

DENNIS SMITH

Pacific Press®
Publishing Association
Nampa, Idaho | Oshawa, Ontario, Canada
www.pacificpress.com

Edited by Jeannette R. Johnson
Copyedited by Kathy Pepper
Cover design by Ron Pride
Interior design by Patricia S. Wegh
Typeset: Times New Roman 12/16

Smith, Dennis Edwin, 1944–
40 days : prayers and devotions to prepare for the Second Coming / Dennis Smith.
p. cm.
ISBN 978-0-8163-6226-4
1. Second Advent—Prayers and devotions. I. Title. II. Title: Forty days.
BT886.3.S65 2009
242'.2—dc22
2009012475

January 2019

Contents

Introduction

This 40-days-of-study-and-prayer devotional is designed to prepare God's church for Christ's second coming, as well as to reach out to others in preparation for that glorious event. This preparation begins with church members who are willing to commit to 40 days of prayer and devotional study to develop a closer personal relationship with Jesus Christ, and to reach out to five individuals who the Lord has put on their heart to pray for every day.

Jesus said, "If two of you shall agree on earth as touching any thing that they shall ask, it shall be done for them of my Father which is in heaven" (Matt. 18:19). There is great power in united prayer, and there is encouragement and spiritual strength in Christian fellowship. It is suggested that you find a prayer partner to fellowship and pray with, either on the phone or in person, every day during the 40 days of prayer and study.

To gain the greatest benefit, I recommend that you find several individuals to join with you in using this devotional book. It would be well to meet weekly as a group to share and pray together. Choose one in the group to become your daily fellowship-prayer partner. Each participant in the group will do the same so that he/she may receive the greatest blessings during the 40 days.

These devotional studies, selections from five books I have written on these subjects with similar titles, are divided into five sections, with eight devotionals in each section:

- The Baptism of the Holy Spirit
- Spirit Baptism and Prayer
- Spirit Baptism and Evangelism
- Spirit Baptism and Abiding in Christ
- Spirit Baptism and Fellowship

Each devotional study is followed by personal reflection and discussion questions, and a prayer focus for the day, which includes a "prayer verse."

If you want to develop a closer relationship with Jesus and reach out to those whom God has put on your heart who have either once known the truth of God's Word and have slipped away, or have never known the warning message God is giving to prepare the world for Christ's soon return, this book is for you. Those on your prayer list may be family members, friends, or coworkers. A daily prayer list page (Appendix A) is provided for this purpose. During the 40 days you will pray for them every day and prayerfully use the "Activities to Show You Care" (Appendix B) list to determine what the Lord wants you to do to reach out to those for whom you are praying. Appendix C, "Suggested Greeting for Prayer Contact," is helpful when you call those on your prayer list to let them know you will be praying for them during the next 40 days, and ask them what they'd like you to pray for on their behalf.

Prayer is the most powerful force on earth. It is essential for one's personal spiritual growth and is the most effective means of reaching others for Christ. Concerning prayer and the Christian's spiritual growth, Ellen White wrote:

"Prayer is the breath of the soul. It is the secret of spiritual power. No other means of grace can be substituted, and the health of the soul be preserved. Prayer brings the heart into immediate contact with the Wellspring of life, and strengthens the sinew and muscle of the religious experience. Neglect the exercise of prayer, or engage in prayer spasmodically, now and then, as seems convenient, and you lose your hold on God. The spiritual faculties lose their vitality, the religious experience lacks health and vigor" *(Gospel Workers,* p. 254).

Mrs. White also recognized the necessity of prayer in leading others to Christ:

"Through much prayer you must labor for souls, for this is the only method by which you can reach hearts. It is not your work, but the work of Christ who is by your side, that impresses hearts" *(Evangelism,* p. 341).

"The Lord will hear our prayers for the conversion of souls" *(Messages to Young People,* p. 315).

As you prayerfully consider the suggested ways to reach out to those for whom you are praying you will not only be praying for them, you will also be working to bring them closer to Christ and His church. God will bless your efforts when you pray for, and work for, those on your prayer list. He will not only use you to win others to Christ; He will draw you closer to Himself. Ellen White understood this double blessing when she wrote:

"As you work to answer your own prayers, you will find that God will reveal Himself unto you. . . . Begin now to reach higher and still higher. Prize the things of heaven above earthly attractions and inducements. . . . Learn how to pray; learn how to bear a clear and intelligent testimony, and God will be glorified in you" *(The Upward Look,* p. 256).

"Daily He received a fresh baptism of the Holy Spirit"

"Their persevering prayers will bring souls to the cross. In cooperation with their self-sacrificing efforts Jesus will move upon hearts, working miracles in the conversion of souls" *(Testimonies for the Church*, vol. 7, p. 27).

To facilitate the prayer emphasis there is a "Prayer Activity" section at the end of each day's devotional which offers a suggested prayer focus for the day, and incorporates Bible verses to include in your prayer. Many verses in the Bible contain a promise and the condition required for the fulfillment of the promise. When you pray these Bible verses you should do two things:

1. ask God to fulfill the condition (both in you and in the church) that is required for the fulfillment of the promise, and
2. ask God to fulfill the promise.

In the verses and prayer requests section for the "Prayer Activity":

The regular type gives the verses that contain both the promise and the condition of fulfillment, and the *italicized* type gives an example of a prayer you can use to pray the verse, asking God to fulfill the condition, and then asking God to fulfill the promise.

After His resurrection, Jesus told His disciples that they were to wait to receive the baptism of the Holy Spirit before they went forth to proclaim the gospel to the world:

"And, being assembled together with them, commanded them that they should not depart from Jerusalem, but wait for the promise of the Father, which, saith he, ye have heard of me. For John truly baptized with water; but ye shall be baptized with the Holy Ghost not many days hence. . . . But ye shall receive power, after that the Holy Ghost is come upon you: and ye shall be witnesses unto me both in Jerusalem, and in all Judaea, and in Samaria, and unto the uttermost part of the earth" (Acts 1:4-8).

Even though they had spent the past three and a half years daily with Christ and had seen and participated in a ministry of miracles, they were not ready to witness for Him. They were to wait to receive the *power.* After they received the baptism of the Holy Spirit, which took place on the day of Pentecost, they would be empowered as never before to witness for Christ:

"And when the day of Pentecost was fully come, they were all with one accord in one place. And suddenly there came a sound from heaven as of a rushing mighty wind, and it filled all the house where they were sitting.

And there appeared unto them cloven tongues like as of fire, and it sat upon each of them. And they were all filled with the Holy Ghost, and began to speak with other tongues, as the Spirit gave them utterance" (Acts 2:1-4).

Because the baptism of the Holy Spirit (also called the infilling of the Spirit) is so vital to our personal spiritual growth and our witness to others, these 40 devotional lessons will be based on this important teaching in God's Word. You will have the opportunity to better understand the biblical teaching on baptism of the Holy Spirit, as well as enter more fully into this Spirit-filled experience.

By choosing to participate in 40 days of study and prayer, you are entering into an amazing and blessed adventure with the Lord. You will experience a deeper relationship with Christ, and you will see the Lord use you to draw others closer to Himself in preparation for His soon return. As you fellowship with your prayer partner and the others participating in the 40 days of prayer and devotional study, you will experience a deeper Christian love and unity with your fellow believers. This will play an important role in your personal spiritual growth.

In order to get the most from this experience, it is recommended that this be the first thing you do in the morning. It may require rising a little earlier, but the effort will be well rewarded! If you ask the Lord to wake you so you can have some quality time with Him, He will hear and answer your prayer. Concerning Christ's devotional life Ellen White wrote:

"Daily He received a fresh baptism of the Holy Spirit. In the early hours of the new day the Lord awakened Him from His slumbers, and His soul and His lips were anointed with grace, that He might impart to others. His words were given Him fresh from the heavenly courts, words that He might speak in season to the weary and oppressed" *(Christ's Object Lessons,* p. 139).

Christ will do the same for you, if you ask Him. He very much desires to anoint you with His Spirit in preparation for each new day. This book is designed to facilitate just that—a daily anointing of God's Spirit for personal spiritual growth, and witnessing for Christ.

If you are using this devotional study in preparation for a Visitor's Sabbath and/or Evangelistic Meetings at the end of the 40 days, those programs should be included in the prayer focus each day of the 40 days. A 40 Days Instruction Manual is available on the website; www.40daysdevotional.com, to help facilitate a 40 day program in a church setting. Many churches are using this devotional book in this manner, and it is proving to be an effective spiritual preparation for evangelistic meetings as well as increase visitor attendance on Visitor's Sabbath and Evangelistic Meetings held at the conclusion of the 40 days.

Note: 40 DAYS *is designed also to work along with "Light America Mission," a program of personal spiritual growth through the study of God's Word, prayer, training, and community outreach to share the three angels' messages.*

Information on how to conduct a 40 days program of devotional study and prayer in your church is available at www.40daysdevotional.com. A free downloadable Instruction Manual is located on the website.

*"If ye then,
being evil, know how
to give good gifts unto
your children:
how much more shall
your heavenly Father
give the Holy Spirit to
them that ask him?"
(Luke 11:13).*

Day 1

Two Works of the Holy Spirit

The concept of the baptism of the Holy Spirit is that there are two works of the Spirit: one is to lead us to accept Christ and be baptized in water. This work of the Spirit is for everyone.

The second work of the Spirit is to fill the Christian with His presence so he or she can truly live the Christian life and do the works of God. This is the baptism of the Holy Spirit, and this work of the Spirit is not for the unbeliever—only the believer in Jesus Christ. For Jesus said the world cannot receive Him in this manner:

"And I will pray the Father, and he shall give you another Comforter, that he may abide with you for ever; even the Spirit of truth; whom the world cannot receive, because it seeth him not, neither knoweth him: but ye know him; for he dwelleth with you, and shall be in you" (John 14:16, 17).

Jesus indicated that on, and after, the Day of Pentecost the baptism of the Holy Spirit became available to every believer when He said that He "shall be in you." This wonderful infilling-of-the-Spirit experience is available to you today.

Jesus is our example in all things. He was "born" of the Spirit, led by the Spirit from childhood into manhood, and baptized in water. Soon after His water baptism, He was baptized with the Holy Spirit, which He had prayed for at the time of His water baptism:

"Now when all the people were baptized, it came to pass, that Jesus also being baptized, and praying, the heaven was opened, and the Holy Ghost descended in a bodily shape like a dove upon him, and a voice came from heaven, which said, Thou art my beloved Son; in thee I am well pleased" (Luke 3:21, 22).

After the Spirit's infilling He was prepared to go forth in the power of the Spirit to do battle with Satan as never before:

"And Jesus being full of the Holy Ghost returned from Jordan, and was led by the Spirit into the wilderness, being forty days tempted of the devil. And in those days he did eat nothing: and when they were ended, he afterward hungered. And the devil said unto him, If thou be the Son of God, command this stone that it be made bread. And Jesus answered him, saying, It is written, That man shall not live by bread alone, but by every word of God. And the devil, taking him up into an high mountain, shewed unto him all the kingdoms of the world in a moment of time. And the devil said unto him, All this power will I give thee, and the glory of them: for that is delivered unto me; and to whomsoever I will I give it. If thou therefore wilt worship me, all shall be thine. And Jesus answered and said unto him, Get thee behind me, Satan: for it is written, Thou shalt worship the Lord thy God, and him only shalt thou serve. And he brought him to Jerusalem, and set him on a pinnacle of the temple, and said unto him, If thou be the Son of God, cast thyself down from hence: for it is written, He shall give his angels charge over thee, to keep thee: and in their hands they shall bear thee up, lest at any time thou dash thy foot against a stone. And Jesus answering said unto him, It is said, Thou shalt not tempt the Lord thy God. And when the devil had ended all the temptation, he departed from him for a season" (Luke 4:1-13).

He was empowered to preach and teach the kingdom of God, carry on a ministry of healing, and cast out devils:

"And Jesus returned in the power of the Spirit into

Galilee: and there went out a fame of him through all the region round about. . . . The Spirit of the Lord is upon me, because he hath anointed me to preach the gospel to the poor; he hath sent me to heal the brokenhearted, to preach deliverance to the captives, and recovering of sight to the blind, to set at liberty them that are bruised, to preach the acceptable year of the Lord" (verses 14-19).

Jesus said all who believe on Him would do even greater works than He did:

"Verily, verily, I say unto you, He that believeth on me, the works that I do shall he do also; and greater works than these shall he do; because I go unto my Father" (John 14:12).

When believers receive the baptism of the Holy Spirit, they are empowered to do the same works as Christ because the same Spirit that filled Christ has filled them:

"He that believeth on me, as the scripture hath said, out of his belly shall flow rivers of living water. (But this spake he of the Spirit, which they that believe on him should receive: for the Holy Ghost was not yet given; because that Jesus was not yet glorified)" (John 7:38, 39).

Before experiencing this Spirit infilling, God is with the believer because He called and led him to accept Christ and be baptized in water. However, he will not have the fullness of the Spirit's power within him until he receives the baptism of the Holy Spirit. That is why Jesus told the disciples to wait for the outpouring of the Spirit on the day of Pentecost before they went forth to preach the gospel:

"And, being assembled together with them, commanded them that they should not depart from Jerusalem, but wait for the promise of the Father, which, saith he, ye have heard of me. For John truly baptized with water; but ye shall be baptized with the Holy Ghost not many days hence. . . . But ye shall receive power, after that the Holy Ghost is come upon you: and ye shall be witnesses unto me both in Jerusalem, and in all Judaea, and in Samaria, and unto the uttermost part of the earth" (Acts 1:4-8).

The baptism of the Holy Spirit is available to every Christian today. God has promised to give the Spirit in fullness to us if we ask in faith:

"If ye then, being evil, know how to give good gifts unto your children: how much more shall your heavenly Father give the Holy Spirit to them that ask him?" (Luke 11:13).

"That the blessing of Abraham might come on the Gentiles through Jesus Christ; that we might receive the promise of the Spirit through faith" (Gal. 3:14).

Concerning the baptism of the Holy Spirit, Ellen White wrote: "I would that we had the baptism of the Holy Spirit, and this we must have before we can reveal perfection of life and character. I would that each member of the church would open the heart to Jesus, saying, 'Come, heavenly Guest, abide with me'" (2 *Manuscript Release* 26).

Some may question: Do I qualify to receive the baptism of the Holy Spirit? There are two requirements. The first is to have received Christ as your Savior. The second is a decision to commit your life fully to Him. If you have accepted Christ and desire to follow Him in every aspect of your life, you qualify. If this is your desire and you want to experience the baptism of the Holy Spirit, I invite you to pray the following prayer:

Father, I thank You for leading me to accept Jesus Christ as my Savior, and I ask You to forgive me for all my sins. I desire to commit my life 100 percent to Jesus. I thank You for the promise to fill me with Your Spirit and claim the promise of the baptism of the Holy Spirit in my life right now. Father, fill me with Your Spirit and manifest in me every fruit of the Spirit. I pray that You will so infill me with the presence of Jesus that His character will be fully manifested through me. I claim Your promise to empower me by Your Spirit to serve You as You lead me into ministry for Jesus. In Jesus' name, amen."

Personal Reflection and Discussion

What are the two works of the Holy Spirit?

____

____

Who qualifies to receive the baptism of the Holy Spirit?

____

____

List two benefits of receiving the baptism of the Holy Spirit.

____

____

Do you want to receive the baptism of the Holy Spirit, and receive the benefits of the Spirit's infilling in your life and service for the Lord?

____

Prayer Activity

Prayerfully consider what you can do to show you care for those on your prayer list.

Call each of them, telling them that you are praying for them, and ask them what they want you to pray for on their behalf.

Decide who you want to be in fellowship with as you pray during the 40 days of prayer.

Call your prayer partner and discuss this devotional with him/her.

Pray with your prayer partner:

- **for God to baptize each of you with His Holy Spirit.**
- **for God to open your understanding as you study your daily devotional.**
- **for God to bless you and your prayer partner's fellowship.**
- **for the individuals on your prayer list.**

INCLUDE THE FOLLOWING BIBLE VERSE IN YOUR PRAYER:

"I will instruct thee and teach thee in the way which thou shalt go: I will guide thee with mine eye" (Ps. 32:8).

Guide and teach us, Lord, that we will be constantly under Your direction in our lives and church.

Day 2

Receiving Spirit Baptism After Pentecost

Jesus promised to baptize His followers with the Holy Spirit so that they would be empowered to take the gospel to the world:

"And, being assembled together with them, commanded them that they should not depart from Jerusalem, but wait for the promise of the Father, which, saith he, ye have heard of me. For John truly baptized with water; but ye shall be baptized with the Holy Ghost not many days hence. . . . But ye shall receive power, after that the Holy Ghost is come upon you: and ye shall be witnesses unto me both in Jerusalem, and in all Judaea, and in Samaria, and unto the uttermost part of the earth" (Acts 1:4-8).

This promise was fulfilled on the day of Pentecost:

"And when the day of Pentecost was fully come, they were all with one accord in one place. And suddenly there came a sound from heaven as of a rushing mighty wind, and it filled all the house where they were sitting. And there appeared unto them cloven tongues like as of fire, and it sat upon each of them. And they were all filled with the Holy Ghost, and began to speak with other tongues, as the Spirit gave them utterance" (Acts 2:1-4).

The baptism of the Holy Spirit was not only for the disciples at Pentecost; this experience was, and is, for all Christians since that time.

Not every believer was present at Pentecost. A practical question might be, How did Christians receive the baptism of the Spirit after Pentecost? The answer is found in the book of Acts. On at least two occasions the Spirit fell on a group while Peter spoke to them:

"While Peter yet spake these words, the Holy Ghost fell on all them which heard the word. And they of the circumcision which believed were astonished, as many as came with Peter, because that on the Gentiles also was poured out the gift of the Holy Ghost. For they heard them speak with tongues, and magnify God. Then answered Peter, Can any man forbid water, that these should not be baptized, which have received the Holy Ghost as well as we?" (Acts 10:44-47).

"And as I began to speak, the Holy Ghost fell on them, as on us at the beginning. Then remembered I the word of the Lord, how that he said, John indeed baptized with water; but ye shall be baptized with the Holy Ghost. Forasmuch then as God gave them the like gift as he did unto us, who believed on the Lord Jesus Christ; what was I, that I could withstand God?" (Acts 11:15-17).

It appears that God also led the church to receive the baptism of the Spirit in a more orderly way by the laying on of hands. Concerning Samaritan believers receiving the baptism of the Holy Spirit, we read:

"But when they believed Philip preaching the things concerning the kingdom of God, and the name of Jesus Christ, they were baptized, both men and women. Then Simon himself believed also: and when he was baptized, he continued with Philip, and wondered, beholding the miracles and signs which were done. Now when the apostles which were at Jerusalem heard that Samaria had received the word of God, they sent unto them Peter and John: who, when they were come down, prayed for them, that they might receive the Holy Ghost: (For as yet he was fallen upon none of them: only they were baptized in the name of the Lord Jesus.) Then laid they their hands on them, and they received the Holy Ghost" (Acts 8:12-17).

Note that in Acts 8 the individuals of Samaria were led by the Spirit to accept Christ and be baptized in water. Yet they had not received the baptism of the Holy Spirit when they were baptized in water. Peter and John came to them from Jerusalem for the specific purpose of laying hands on them and praying for the baptism of the Spirit to come upon them. This is a clear indication that water baptism and Spirit baptism are two separate experiences. The Spirit leads an individual to accept Christ and be baptized in water. This is a different work of the Spirit than the baptism of the Spirit, which must be sought separately when one becomes aware of this wonderful experience.

We see in Acts that Saul, who later became the apostle Paul, also received the baptism of the Spirit by prayer and the laying on of hands:

"And Ananias went his way, and entered into the house; and putting his hands on him said, Brother Saul, the Lord, even Jesus, that appeared unto thee in the way as thou camest, hath sent me, that thou mightest receive thy sight, and be filled with the Holy Ghost. And immediately there fell from his eyes as it had been scales: and he received sight forthwith, and arose, and was baptized" (Acts 9:17, 18).

In Saul's case the baptism of the Holy Spirit came soon after his conversion on the road to Damascus but before his water baptism.

We find a similar example of prayer with laying on of hands when Paul met with disciples in Ephesus:

"And it came to pass, that, while Apollos was at Corinth, Paul having passed through the upper coasts came to Ephesus: and finding certain disciples, he said unto them, Have ye received the Holy Ghost since ye believed? And they said unto him, We have not so much as heard whether there be any Holy Ghost. And he said unto them, Unto what then were ye baptized? And they said, Unto John's baptism. Then said Paul, John verily baptized with the baptism of repentance, saying unto the people, that they should believe on him which should come after him, that is, on Christ Jesus. When they heard this, they were baptized in the name of the Lord Jesus. And when Paul had laid his hands upon them, the Holy Ghost came on them; and they spake with tongues, and prophesied (Acts 19:1-6).

The one performing this prayer with laying on of hands should be a believer who has received the baptism of the Holy Spirit themselves. It should also be pointed out that the laying on of hands is not necessary to receive the baptism of the Holy Spirit. It is a wonderful experience to seek the Spirit's infilling in this manner; however, it is not necessary. Receiving the baptism of the Spirit is simply a matter of claiming by faith God's promise of the Spirit:

"That the blessing of Abraham might come on the Gentiles through Jesus Christ; that we might receive the promise of the Spirit through faith" (Gal. 3:14).

Ellen White understood that Christians do not automatically receive the baptism of the Holy Spirit at conversion or when baptized in water. Of our great need for the Spirit's infilling in order to witness to others effectively, she wrote:

"What we need is the baptism of the Holy Spirit. Without this, we are no more fitted to go forth to the world than were the disciples after the crucifixion of their Lord" (Review and Herald, Feb. 18, 1890).

Concerning our personal spiritual growth and the Spirit's infilling, she wrote:

Jesus promised to baptize His followers with the Holy Spirit so they would be empowered to take the gospel to the world

"Impress upon all the necessity of the baptism of the Holy Spirit, the sanctification of the members of the church, so that they will be living, growing, fruit-bearing trees of the Lord's planting" (*Testimonies for the Church,* vol. 6, p. 86).

If Christians automatically had the baptism of the Holy Spirit, Mrs. White would not admonish us to receive it. When one reads her statements it is clear that she saw its importance and urged every believer to seek the fullness of the Spirit in his/her life.

Personal Reflection and Discussion

Why did Jesus tell the disciples to wait for the baptism of the Holy Spirit?

When did the disciples receive the baptism of the Holy Spirit?

Did every Christian when they received Christ or were baptized in water, automatically receive the baptism of the Holy Spirit after the day of Pentecost?

How did the Samaritan believers receive the baptism of the Holy Spirit?

When and how did Saul, who later became the apostle Paul, receive the baptism of the Holy Spirit?

What did Ellen White say about the importance of receiving the baptism of the Holy Spirit?

Is prayer with laying on of hands necessary to receive the baptism of the Holy Spirit?

Prayer Activity

Call your prayer partner and discuss this devotional with him/her.
Pray with your prayer partner:

- **for God to continue to baptize each of you with His Holy Spirit.**
- **for God to minister through you in the power of the Spirit.**
- **for individuals on your prayer list.**

INCLUDE THE FOLLOWING BIBLE VERSE IN YOUR PRAYER:
"Remember, O Lord, thy tender mercies and thy lovingkindnesses; for they have been ever of old" (Ps. 25:6).

Be merciful to us and forgive us our sins.
Restore us to Your favor and glorify Your name through us.

Benefits of Receiving the Baptism of the Spirit

What happens when we ask God for the baptism of the Holy Spirit? A few examples of the changes the infilling of the Spirit will bring to the life of the receiver are: (1) a stronger desire to study God's Word, (2) a more earnest prayer life, (3) a deeper repentance for our sins, and (4) changes in lifestyles and activities.

The infilling of the Spirit is necessary for the believer to walk victoriously in Christ. According to the Bible, one does not "know" Christ in the fullest, biblical sense without the baptism of the Holy Spirit. This is illustrated in the parable of the ten virgins (Matt. 25:1-13), in which Christ told the foolish virgins, who were without the oil of the Holy Spirit, "I know you not" (verse 12).

Here, as well as in other Scriptures, Christ speaks of not "knowing" someone. For example, Jesus said:

"Not every one that saith unto me, Lord, Lord, shall enter into the kingdom of heaven; but he that doeth the will of my Father which is in heaven. Many will say to me in that day, Lord, Lord, have we not prophesied in thy name? and in thy name have cast out devils? and in thy name done many wonderful works? And then will I profess unto them, I never knew you: depart from me, ye that work iniquity" (Matt. 7:21-23).

Simply knowing the teachings of the Bible, or engaging in active ministry for Jesus, is not a substitute for knowing Him intimately through the baptism of the Holy Spirit.

Water baptism is similar to the wedding service, while Spirit baptism is symbolized by the consummation of the marriage when the bride "knows" her bridegroom. Satan will resist this work fiercely; for he is aware that the Spirit's infilling will break his power in the believer's life.

Understanding and experiencing the infilling of the Holy Spirit is second in importance only to understanding and accepting Christ as our Savior. Nor is there any more important work for the believer than to seek the Spirit's infilling and to learn to walk victoriously in the Spirit.

Another very important point is that we must renew this infilling every day. It is not a "once and forever" experience. Paul tells us that "the inward man is renewed day by day" (2 Cor. 4:16). We need the renewing of the Spirit every day of our lives. Paul's command to "be filled with the Spirit" (Eph. 5:18) is a continuous action verb in the Greek meaning; we are to keep on being filled with the Spirit daily.

Christ is our example in all things. Of Christ's Spirit-baptized experience Ellen White writes:

"Daily He received a fresh baptism of the Holy Spirit. In the early hours of the new day the Lord awakened Him from His slumbers, and His soul and His lips were anointed with grace, that He might impart to others" (*Christ's Object Lessons,* p. 139).

If Christ needed to receive the baptism of the Spirit every day, the Christian surely needs to pray for this daily experience in the Spirit.

Our growth into the fullness of Christ by the Spirit is a process:

"But we all, with open face beholding as in a glass the glory of the Lord, are changed into the same image from glory to glory, even as by the Spirit of the Lord" (2 Cor. 3:18).

Spiritual growth is a process into which we must enter anew every day. Ellen White described the development of character the recipient of the Spirit's infilling receives when she wrote:

"When the Spirit of God takes possession of the heart, it transforms the life. Sinful thoughts are put away, evil deeds are renounced; love, humility, and peace take the place of anger, envy, and strife. Joy takes the place of sadness, and the countenance reflects the light of heaven" (*The Desire of Ages,* p. 173).

What a wonderful blessing our Lord has provided for each of us through the baptism of the Holy Spirit!

Personal Reflection and Discussion

List four benefits of receiving the baptism of the Holy Spirit.

____

Is the baptism of the Spirit to be a one-time event in the Christian's life?

____

How often is the Christian to receive the baptism of the Holy Spirit?

____

How often did Christ receive the baptism of the Holy Spirit?

____

What does receiving the baptism of the Holy Spirit do for our relationship with Christ?

____

Why is Satan fearful of your receiving the Spirit's infilling?

____

What does Ellen White say will happen in our life when we receive the baptism of the Holy Spirit?

____

Prayer Activity

Call your prayer partner to discuss this devotional with him/her.
Pray with your prayer partner:

- **for God to continue to baptize each of you with His Holy Spirit.**
- **for Christ to manifest the changes in your life necessary for you to reflect Him fully.**
- **for the individuals on your prayer list.**

INCLUDE THE FOLLOWING BIBLE VERSE IN YOUR PRAYER:
"Behold, the eye of the Lord is upon them that fear him, upon them that hope in his mercy; to deliver their soul from death, and to keep them alive in famine. Our soul waiteth for the Lord: he is our help and our shield. For our heart shall rejoice in him, because we have trusted in his holy name. Let thy mercy, O Lord, be upon us, according as we hope in thee" (Ps. 33:18-22).

Turn our hope to You, Lord, and not to earthly things.
Deliver us from our spiritually dead condition.
Bring us back to spiritual life, from our condition of spiritual famine.
Be our help and shield—cause us to rejoice in You.

Day 4

Christ In You

When the believer receives the baptism of the Holy Spirit, he is actually receiving Christ more fully into his life. Jesus foretold this when He promised His disciples another Comforter that the Father would send to dwell with them and "be in" them:

"And I will pray the Father, and he shall give you another Comforter, that he may abide with you for ever; Even the Spirit of truth; whom the world cannot receive, because it seeth him not, neither knoweth him: but ye know him; for he dwelleth with you, and shall be in you" (John 14:16, 17.)

This Comforter is the Holy Spirit. Then Jesus said:

"I will not leave you comfortless: I will come to you" (verse 18).

Hence, through the Holy Spirit Jesus comes to "dwell with" and "be in" His people. It is through the Spirit's infilling that Jesus most fully lives within His disciples:

"And he that keepeth his commandments dwelleth in him, and he in him. And hereby we know that he abideth in us, by the Spirit which he hath given us" (1 John 3:24).

John tells us that the Christians who are living when Jesus comes will be "like" Jesus:

"Beloved, now are we the sons of God, and it doth not yet appear what we shall be: but we know that, when he shall appear, we shall be like him; for we shall see him as he is" (verse 2).

How much like Jesus are we to become? The Greek word translated "like" means "just like" Him. How can this happen? Through the daily baptism of the Holy Spirit, Jesus will live out His life in us. Paul described this when he wrote:

"I am crucified with Christ: nevertheless I live; yet not I, but Christ liveth in me: and the life which I now live in the flesh I live by the faith of the Son of God, who loved me, and gave himself for me" (Gal. 2:20).

Through the infilling of the Holy Spirit, Christ will come and live in each of us. Because of Christ's indwelling presence the Spirit-filled believer will have the mind of Christ:

"For who hath known the mind of the Lord, that he may instruct him? But we have the mind of Christ" (1 Cor. 2:16).

"Let this mind be in you, which was also in Christ Jesus" (Phil. 2:5).

Believers will have the likes and dislikes of Christ—the love of righteousness and sanctification, and hatred of sin. They will have the same desire to obey the Father that Christ has:

"Then said I, Lo, I come: in the volume of the book it is written of me, I delight to do thy will, O my God: yea, thy law is within my heart" (Ps. 40:7, 8).

The same passion for souls that Christ has will be in them:

"For the Son of man is come to seek and to save that which was lost" (Luke 19:10).

Paul tells us the wisdom (righteousness) and holiness of Christ is theirs:

"That no flesh should glory in his presence. But of him are ye in Christ Jesus, who of God is made unto us wisdom, and righteousness, and sanctification, and redemption: That, according as it is written, He that glorieth, let him glory in the Lord" (1 Cor. 1:29-31).

Every virtue and quality of Christ dwells in the Spirit-filled believer because Christ dwells in them. Paul indicated this when he wrote, 'Christ is being formed in you.' Gal. 4:19. They will become more and more like Christ every day as they are changed into His image "from glory to glory, even as by the Spirit of the Lord" (2 Cor. 3:18).

Christ living in the believer through the infilling of the Spirit causes the character of Christ to be fully developed in them. The Holy Spirit brings the "fruit of the Spirit" with Him:

"But the fruit of the Spirit is love, joy, peace, longsuffering, gentleness, goodness, faith, meekness, temperance: against such there is no law" (Gal. 5:22, 23).

These wonderful fruits of character will be manifested in the life more and more abundantly as the Spirit takes a fuller possession of the life. The Spirit will take such control of the believer that they will become like Jesus in every way (1 John 3:2).

The baptism of the Holy Spirit will also bring about the fulfillment of Christ's promise that the believers would do the "works" He did, and greater works:

"Verily, verily, I say unto you, He that believeth on me, the works that I do shall he do also; and greater works than these shall he do; because I go unto my Father" (John 14:12).

This happens when the believer receives the baptism of the Holy Spirit and continues to walk in the Spirit. In a very real sense every believer becomes as Christ to the world. We become Christ's mouth, hands, and feet, doing the very works He did—preaching, teaching, healing, casting out devils—every work Jesus did.

It is this full "manifestation of the sons of God" that the whole of creation is waiting for:

"For the earnest expectation of the creature waiteth for the manifestation of the sons of God" (Rom. 8:19).

When this occurs in its fullness, the earth will then be lighted with God's character of glory and the end will come:

"And after these things I saw another angel come down from heaven, having great power; and the earth was lightened with his glory" (Rev. 18:1).

Christ's presence dwelling in the believer through the baptism of the Holy Spirit is the Christian's only hope of His glory being revealed in, and through, them:

"To whom God would make known what is the riches of the glory of this mystery among the Gentiles; which is Christ in you, the hope of glory" (Col. 1:27).

Personal Reflection and Discussion

When the believer receives the baptism of the Holy Spirit, who else does he receive?

____

What benefits does the Christian receive when Christ dwells in him/her through the baptism of the Holy Spirit?

____

____

____

____

What is the whole of creation waiting for?

____

Prayer Activity

Call your prayer partner and discuss this devotional with him/her.
Pray with your prayer partner:

- **for God to continue to baptize each of you with His Holy Spirit.**
- **for Christ to live in you fully, and manifest His character and works in you.**
- **for the individuals on your prayer list.**

INCLUDE THE FOLLOWING BIBLE VERSE IN YOUR PRAYER:
"The righteous cry, and the Lord heareth, and delivereth them out of all their troubles" (Ps. 34:17).

Hear us and deliver us from the things that hinder us from growing fully in Christ, individually, and as a congregation.

Day 5

Spirit Baptism and Obedience

There are two purposes for the baptism of the Holy Spirit. One is to reflect Jesus fully in our life:

"Forasmuch as ye are manifestly declared to be the epistle of Christ ministered by us, written not with ink, but with the Spirit of the living God; not in tables of stone, but in fleshly tables of the heart" (2 Cor. 3:3).

God's goal is that Christ be seen in us; that we be a living letter revealing the character of Christ.

The second purpose of the Spirit's infilling is to receive a power for witnessing:

"But ye shall receive power, after that the Holy Ghost is come upon you: and ye shall be witnesses unto me both in Jerusalem, and in all Judaea, and in Samaria, and unto the uttermost part of the earth" (Acts 1:8).

In today's devotional we will focus on the first purpose—reflecting Jesus' character.

The Holy Spirit was very much involved when God gave the Ten Commandments to Moses. In fact, it was the Spirit who wrote the commandments on the tables of stone. This becomes clear when we compare Jesus' statements in which He equates the "finger of God" with the "Spirit of God":

"But if I cast out devils by the Spirit of God, then the kingdom of God is come unto you" (Matt. 12:28).

"But if I with the finger of God cast out devils, no doubt the kingdom of God is come upon you" (Luke 11:20).

Hence, the same Holy Spirit who wrote the Ten Commandments on tables of stone will today write God's law on the heart of God's Spirit-filled children:

"Forasmuch as ye are manifestly declared to be the epistle of Christ ministered by us, written not with ink, but with the Spirit of the living God; not in tables of stone, but in fleshly tables of the heart" (2 Cor. 3:3).

The professed Christian can participate in two kinds of obedience. First is what I call *external* obedience. This obedience occurs when the believer obeys the law of God simply because God says to obey it. This type of obedience is actually legalism, not being from the heart. The second form of obedience is *internal* obedience, and occurs because of a deep, inner desire within the believer to obey God. External obedience without heart obedience is unacceptable to God:

"For thou desirest not sacrifice; else would I give it: thou delightest not in burnt offering. The sacrifices of God are a broken spirit: a broken and a contrite heart, O God, thou wilt not despise" (Ps. 51:16, 17).

"This people draweth nigh unto me with their mouth, and honoureth me with their lips; but their heart is far from me" (Matt. 15:8).

I came across an illustration many years ago that clarifies the difference between external and internal obedience. Let's say my father died, and I'm not sure if I should mourn his death, or not, so I go to a friend and ask his advice. We discuss whether or not I should mourn. My friend finally says, "After all, he was your father, and you are his son. So I think you should mourn his death." On his advice I begin mourning his death. I think it becomes obvious that my mourning in this case would not be genuine mourning from the heart. Rather, it would be external mourning because it was my obligation, as my father's son, to mourn his death. True mourning would come spontaneously from the heart. I couldn't help but mourn if it was genuine mourning. The same is true of obedience to God. When one is in right relationship with God through the infilling of the Spirit, obedience springs naturally and spontaneously from the heart without even thinking about it. Temptations to disobey will come; however, they will be much weakened in influence by the strong desire God has placed in the heart to obey.

Through the baptism, or infilling of the Holy Spirit, God's law is written in our hearts, and we obey from the heart. This does not fully happen when we accept Christ and are baptized by water. Paul states that we must continually be "filled with the Spirit," which is necessary for God's law to continue to be written on our heart:

"And be not drunk with wine, wherein is excess; but be filled with the Spirit" (Eph. 5:18).

Ellen White described this "internal" obedience, which springs from daily experiencing the baptism of the Holy Spirit, when she wrote:

"All true obedience comes from the heart. It was heart work with Christ. And if we consent, He will so identify Himself with our thoughts and aims, so blend our hearts and minds into conformity to His will, that when obeying Him we shall be but carrying out our own impulses. The will, refined and sanctified, will find its highest delight in doing His service. When we know God, as it is our privilege to know Him, our life will be a life of continual obedience. Through an appreciation of the character of Christ, through communion with God, sin will become hateful to us" (*The Desire of Ages,* p. 668).

Personal Reflection and Discussion

What are the two purposes of receiving the baptism of the Holy Spirit?

Which member of the Godhead wrote the Ten Commandments on the tables of stone?

What are the two types of obedience that professed Christians can participate in?

What is the only kind of obedience God accepts?

How does Ellen White describe obedience from the heart?

Prayer Activity

Continue your efforts to contact all on you prayer list this week to tell them you are praying for them, and ask them what they want you to pray for on their behalf.

Call your prayer partner and discuss this devotional with him/her.

Pray with your prayer partner:

- **for God to continue to baptize each of you with His Holy Spirit.**
- **for God to write His law on you heart.**
- **for the individuals on your prayer list.**

INCLUDE THE FOLLOWING BIBLE VERSE IN YOUR PRAYER:

"Create in me a clean heart, O God; and renew a right spirit within me. Cast me not away from thy presence; and take not thy holy spirit from me. Restore unto me the joy of thy salvation; and uphold me with thy free spirit" (Ps. 51:10-12).

Lord, remove from me my sinful heart and prideful spirit.
In mercy bring me close to You, and restore the fullness of Your Spirit to me.
Bring me to experience the full joy of Your salvation, and give me Your strength.

Day 6

Grieving the Holy Spirit

There are things that we can do that will grieve the Spirit:

"And grieve not the holy Spirit of God, whereby ye are sealed unto the day of redemption" (Eph. 4:30).

If we do not daily seek Him and cooperate in following where He leads us, His power will wane and our Christian experience will weaken.

God doesn't force. When we receive the baptism of the Spirit, He will have a greater impact in our life. We will feel His prompting more strongly. He will be daily putting the desire in our heart to obey God. He will call us to study God's Word and to pray more. The Spirit will cause us to begin loving righteousness and hating sin. However, we are always free to disregard His prompting. When we do this we begin the process of "grieving," or "quenching," the Spirit. Paul gives practical advice in many portions of Scripture on how to avoid doing this. These practical counsels to the believer on living the Christian life are intended to help us maintain the fullness of the Spirit in our lives. Two examples of such counsel are found in the following Bible verses:

"And that ye put on the new man, which after God is created in righteousness and true holiness. Wherefore putting away lying, speak every man truth with his neighbour: for we are members one of another. Be ye angry, and sin not: let not the sun go down upon your wrath: Neither give place to the devil. Let him that stole steal no more: but rather let him labour, working with his hands the thing which is good, that he may have to give to him that needeth. Let no corrupt communication proceed out of your mouth, but that which is good to the use of edifying, that it may minister grace unto the hearers. And grieve not the holy Spirit of God, whereby ye are sealed unto the day of redemption. Let all bitterness, and wrath, and anger, and clamour, and evil speaking, be put away from you, with all malice: and be ye kind one to another, tenderhearted, forgiving one another, even as God for Christ's sake hath forgiven you" (Eph. 4:24-32).

"Now we exhort you, brethren, warn them that are unruly, comfort the feebleminded, support the weak, be patient toward all men. See that none render evil for evil unto any man; but ever follow that which is good, both among yourselves, and to all men. Rejoice evermore. Pray without ceasing. In every thing give thanks: for this is the will of God in Christ Jesus concerning you. Quench not the Spirit" (1Thess. 5:14-19).

Paul knew that the Spirit of God dwelling in the believer would be prompting him to do the things listed in these verses. If we refuse to yield to His prompting, though, we will be in danger of grieving and quenching the Spirit.

If you find that you have grieved the Spirit, don't become discouraged! Ask God to forgive you, and He will:

"If we confess our sins, he is faithful and just to forgive us our sins, and to cleanse us from all unrighteousness" (1 John 1:9).

Then ask God in faith to fill you anew with His Spirit, and He will do that too:

"If ye then, being evil, know how to give good gifts unto your children: how much more shall your heavenly Father give the Holy Spirit to them that ask him?" (Luke 11:13).

David knew God's mercy. He had committed the

sins of adultery and murder. He had walked away from the prompting of God's Spirit in his life when he committed these terrible acts. Yet when he was convicted of his sin by the Spirit, he turned to God in prayer. Note especially these words:

"Hide thy face from my sins, and blot out all mine iniquities. Create in me a clean heart, O God; and renew a right spirit within me. Cast me not away from thy presence; and take not thy holy spirit from me. Restore unto me the joy of thy salvation; and uphold me with thy free spirit" (Ps. 51:9-12).

When we find that we've been slipping away from God we must not let another moment go by without confessing our sin, accepting God's forgiveness, and claiming the promise of the renewing of the Spirit in our lives just as David did. Then we will be strengthened once again in the "inner" man to be victorious over Satan:

"That he would grant you, according to the riches of his glory, to be strengthened with might by his Spirit in the inner man; that Christ may dwell in your hearts by faith; that ye, being rooted and grounded in love, may be able to comprehend with all saints what is the breadth, and length, and depth, and height; and to know the love of Christ, which passeth knowledge, that ye might be filled with all the fulness of God" (Eph. 3:16-19).

We serve a wonderful God. When we have failed Him, let us remember:

"The Lord is merciful and gracious, slow to anger, and plenteous in mercy. He will not always chide: neither will he keep his anger for ever. He hath not dealt with us after our sins; nor rewarded us according to our iniquities. For as the heaven is high above the earth, so great is his mercy toward them that fear him. As far as the east is from the west, so far hath he removed our transgressions from us. Like as a father pitieth his children, so the Lord pitieth them that fear him. For he knoweth our frame; he remembereth that we are dust" (Ps. 103:8-14).

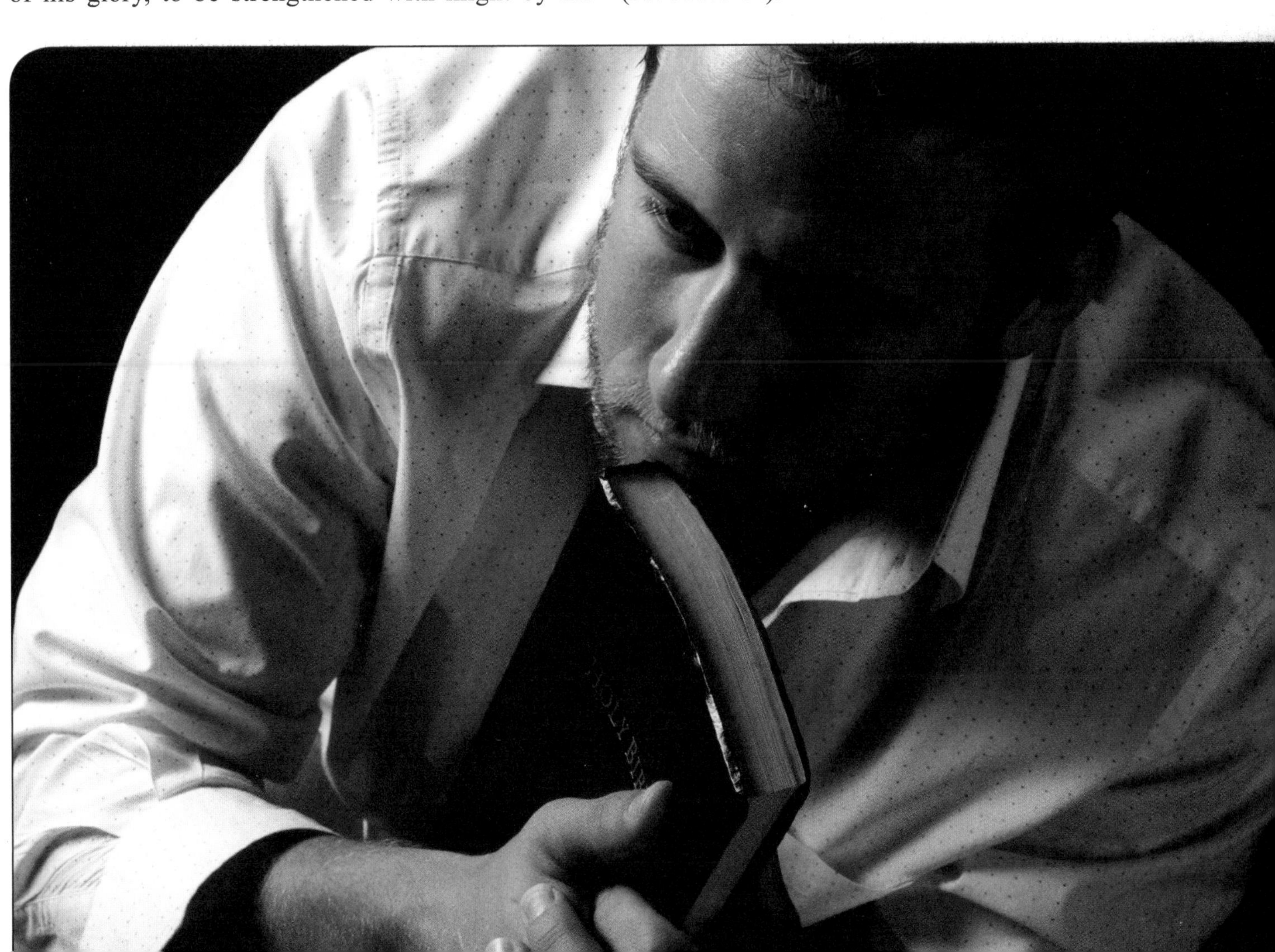

Personal Reflection and Discussion

List some behaviors and attitudes the Holy Spirit will seek to bring into the Christian's life.

____

____

How does a Christian grieve the Holy Spirit?

____

____

If we have grieved the Holy Spirit, what should we do?

____

What is God's attitude toward His children?

____

Prayer Activity

Call your prayer partner and discuss this devotional with him/her.
Pray with your prayer partner:

- **for God to continue to baptize each of you with His Holy Spirit.**
- **for God to forgive you if you have grieved the Holy Spirit in any way.**
- **for God to give you the desire to yield to the Spirit's promptings in your life.**
- **for the individuals on your prayer list.**

INCLUDE THE FOLLOWING BIBLE VERSE IN YOUR PRAYER:
"For the eyes of the Lord run to and fro throughout the whole earth, to show himself strong in behalf of them whose heart is perfect [fully committed (NIV)] (2 Chron. 16:9).

Make our hearts fully committed to You.
Show Yourself strong in our behalf to bring about the needed changes in us that we will experience the revival and reformation we need.

Day 7

Spirit Baptism and the Latter Rain

It is vital that we daily experience the early rain baptism of the Holy Spirit in order to spiritually grow to the point that we will benefit from the latter rain of the Spirit, which prepares the Christian for the final crisis and Christ's return. However, many don't realize this and feel that they must wait for the latter rain of the Spirit if they are finally to have the victory over their besetting sins and spiritual immaturity. Such a view will end in disaster for the one who holds it. Ellen White warns:

"I saw that many were neglecting the preparation so needful, and were looking to the time of 'refreshing' and the 'latter rain' to fit them to stand in the day of the Lord, and to live in His sight. Oh, how many I saw in the time of trouble without a shelter! They had neglected the needful preparation, therefore they could not receive the refreshing that all must have to fit them to live in the sight of a holy God".

We must have victory over all temptation and sin in our life if we are to benefit from the latter rain outpouring of the Spirit. It is a deception of Satan if we believe we do not have to take seriously the sin problem in our lives:

"Repent ye therefore, and be converted, that your sins may be blotted out, when the times of refreshing shall come from the presence of the Lord" (Acts 3:19).

"Knowing this, that our old man is crucified with him, that the body of sin might be destroyed, that henceforth we should not serve sin. . . . Likewise reckon ye also yourselves to be dead indeed unto sin, but alive unto God through Jesus Christ our Lord. Let not sin therefore reign in your mortal body, that ye should obey it in the lusts thereof. Neither yield ye your members as instruments of unrighteousness unto sin: but yield yourselves unto God, as those that are alive from the dead, and your members as instruments of righteousness unto God. For sin shall not have dominion over you: for ye are not under the law, but under grace" (Rom. 6:6, 11-14).

Ellen White confirmed this with these words:

"I saw that none could share the 'refreshing' [latter rain], unless they obtained the victory over every besetment, over pride, selfishness, love of the world, and over every wrong word and action" (*Ibid.*, p. 113).

This may sound impossible to you right now. However, the key to victory over temptation is in learning how to let Jesus live out His life of victory in, and through, us. That wonderful biblical truth will be presented later in this devotional series.

The early, or former rain of the Spirit, which is the baptism of the Holy Spirit, began on the day of Pentecost. Peter pointed this out when he said to the crowd on that day:

"But this is that which was spoken by the prophet Joel; and it shall come to pass in the last days, saith God, I will pour out of my Spirit upon all flesh: and your sons and your daughters shall prophesy, and your young men shall see visions, and your old men shall dream dreams: and on my servants and on my handmaidens I will pour out in those days of my Spirit; and they shall prophesy" (Acts 2:16-18).

Spirit baptism, or the early rain of the Spirit, brings us to the spiritual maturity required so that we can benefit from the latter rain:

"The latter rain, ripening earth's harvest, represents the spiritual grace that prepares the church for the coming of the Son of man. But unless the former rain has fallen, there will be no life; the green blade will not spring up. Unless the early showers have done their work, the latter rain can bring no seed to perfection" (*The Faith I Live By,* p. 333).

Full spiritual growth under the early rain baptism of the Spirit is necessary for us to be able even to recognize the latter rain of the Spirit when it is falling. Ellen White pointed this out when she wrote:

"Unless we are daily advancing in the exemplification of the active Christian virtues, we shall not recognize the manifestations of the Holy Spirit in the latter rain. It may be falling on hearts all around us, but we shall not discern or receive it" (*Testimony to Ministers and Gospel Workers,* p. 507).

If you have not received the baptism of the Holy Spirit don't delay another day. His reception should be first and foremost in our lives, for this Gift will bring all other gifts to us. The Spirit's infilling will enable Christ to live in us and to change our lethargy to excitement, our weakness to strength, and our witness will be with a power not seen since the day of Pentecost:

"I am crucified with Christ: nevertheless I live; yet not I, but Christ liveth in me: and the life which I now live in the flesh I live by the faith of the Son of God, who loved me, and gave himself for me" (Gal. 2:20).

"But ye shall receive power, after that the Holy Ghost is come upon you: and ye shall be witnesses unto me both in Jerusalem, and in all Judaea, and in Samaria, and unto the uttermost part of the earth" (Acts 1:8).

Personal Reflection and Discussion

What are the two outpourings of the Holy Spirit called in the Bible?

When did the early rain of the Spirit begin?

Which "rain of the Spirit" is the baptism of the Holy Spirit?

How necessary is it for the Christian to receive the baptism of the Spirit in order to benefit from the latter rain of the Spirit?

What changes must happen in the Christian's life under the early rain baptism of the Holy Spirit to be ready for the latter rain of the Spirit?

Is it wise to wait for the latter rain before we take the sin problem in our life seriously?

Prayer Activity

Call your prayer partner and discuss this devotional with him/her.
Pray with your prayer partner:

- **for God to continue to baptize each of you with His Holy Spirit.**
- **for God to prepare you to receive the latter rain of the Spirit.**
- **for the individuals on your prayer list.**

INCLUDE THE FOLLOWING BIBLE VERSE IN YOUR PRAYER:
"The angel of the Lord encampeth round about them that fear him, and delivereth them" (Ps. 34:7).

Deliver us from our state of spiritual lethargy and protect us from Satan's attacks.

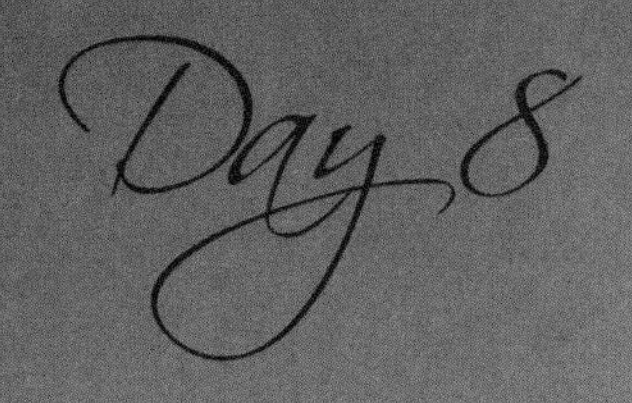

Spirit Baptism and Christ's Return

The good news for today is that Jesus is coming soon! I don't say this only because of terrorist attacks, world conflicts, epidemic outbreaks, or natural disasters—all these certainly indicate Christ's return is soon. However, there is something else that convicts me even more that Christ's coming is imminent. It is His moving among us to understand and to receive the baptism of the Holy Spirit.

The last verses of Revelation 6 describe Jesus' coming and ask the question Who shall be able to stand? meaning, who will be able to survive the event? The answer is found in Revelation 7:1-3.

"And after these things I saw four angels standing on the four corners of the earth, holding the four winds of the earth, that the wind should not blow on the earth, nor on the sea, nor on any tree. And I saw another angel ascending from the east, having the seal of the living God: and he cried with a loud voice to the four angels, to whom it was given to hurt the earth and the sea, Saying, Hurt not the earth, neither the sea, nor the trees, till we have sealed the servants of our God in their foreheads."

Only those who have the seal of God will be able to survive the second coming of Christ. In fact, God is holding back many destructive forces in this earth until God's people are sealed. An important question, then, is how are we sealed? The Bible says we are sealed by the Holy Spirit:

"And grieve not the holy Spirit of God, whereby ye are sealed unto the day of redemption" (Eph. 4:30).

That is what the baptism of the Holy Sprit is all about. It is as we daily receive the baptism of the Holy Spirit that we are sealed and prepared for Christ's second coming.

God is not waiting for more terrorist attacks, disease outbreaks, or natural disasters. Ellen White tells us what Christ is waiting for:

"Christ is waiting with longing desire for the manifestation of Himself in His church. When the character of Christ shall be perfectly reproduced in His people, then He will come to claim them as His own" (*Christ's Object Lessons,* p. 69).

Only by the baptism of the Holy Spirit can this happen in our lives. And only by the baptism of the Holy Spirit can we be ready when the angels let go the winds of destruction. Ellen White writes:

"Nothing but the baptism of the Holy Spirit can bring up the church to its right position, and prepare the people of God for the fast approaching conflict" (*2 Manuscript Releases,* p. 30).

We have a danger, as Seventh-day Adventists. We think we are secure and will be ready for Christ's return because we know about the Sabbath, the state of the dead, the mark of the beast, and the manner of Christ's second coming. This is a deadly error. These teachings are important; however, this knowledge alone will not save us. Remember, it was tithe-paying, Sabbath-keeping, health reformers who crucified Jesus. No; it is not what we know; it is who we know that will enable us to be saved (John 17:3). We must have an intimate relationship with Jesus Christ if we are to be ready for His return.

Today God is calling a people to receive the baptism of the Holy Spirit in preparation for becoming just like Jesus, in order to receive the latter rain of the Spirit, and to be ready for Christ's return:

"Beloved, now are we the sons of God, and it doth

not yet appear what we shall be: but we know that, when he shall appear, we shall be like him; for we shall see him as he is" (1 John 3:2).

However, the church has a problem today. God tells us that we are in a Laodicean condition and, if we don't change, we will not be ready for Christ's return. God also gives us the solution: let Jesus into our lives more fully:

"Behold, I stand at the door, and knock: if any man hear my voice, and open the door, I will come in to him, and will sup with him, and he with me" (Rev. 3:20).

How do we let Jesus in and have the intimate relationship with Him that we must have? Ellen White tells us:

"We must have a living connection with God. We must be clothed with power from on high by the baptism of the Holy Spirit that we may reach a higher standard; for there is help for us in no other way" (*Review and Herald,* April 5, 1892).

Personal Reflection and Discussion

Why are the angels holding back the winds of destruction on this earth?

____

Is knowing the doctrines of the Bible all we need in order to be saved? Why, or why not?

____

According to the Bible, how are we sealed?

____

What does the baptism of the Holy Spirit do for our relationship with Christ?

____

____

What only will prepare us for the final crisis?

____

Prayer Activity

Call your prayer partner and discuss this devotional with him/her.
Pray with your prayer partner:

- **for God to continue to baptize each of you with His Holy Spirit.**
- **for God to prepare you for earth's final crisis and Christ's return.**
- **for the individuals on your prayer list.**

INCLUDE THE FOLLOWING BIBLE VERSE IN YOUR PRAYER:
"The Lord is nigh unto them that are of a broken heart; and saveth such as be of a contrite spirit" (Ps. 34:18).

Cause us to be broken of our pride and put a contrite spirit in us.
Save us from our sinful ways and heal our spiritual backsliding.

A Spirit-given Desire to Pray

When we receive the baptism of the Holy Spirit a deep, inner desire will begin to develop within us to be more in prayer to our heavenly Father:

"And I will pour upon the house of David, and upon the inhabitants of Jerusalem, the spirit of grace and of supplications" (Zech. 12:10).

We can either yield to this God-given desire, or ignore it and continue being more of an active Christian than a praying Christian. However, if we want to experience the deep things of God and the fullness of Christ in our lives, we must yield to this desire to pray. If we want to see His delivering power manifested in our lives over everything Satan tries to bring on us and to see the power of God manifested through us in blessing others with His deliverance, we must spend much time with God in prayer.

Christians have known the importance of prayer for years. Many times we have made efforts to take time in prayer, but those special seasons of prayer were motivated by some crisis and didn't continue for very long. Our problem is that we've become very self-sufficient in meeting our own needs and the needs of the church. We have learned to rely on our own efforts to do the work of God. We have been involved in much planning and many programs. We have learned to depend on the "flesh" to do God's work. In mercy, He has blessed our feeble efforts. However, a blessing beyond our greatest expectations awaits us when we receive the baptism of the Holy Spirit and enter into the prayer relationship He desires for us. Only then will our plans be God's plans, and our activities be God's activities.

Jesus had this kind of meaningful, deep, and powerful relationship with His Father. In fact, this relationship was so close and intimate that Jesus said:

"I and my Father are one" (John 10:30).

Everything Jesus did was under the direction of His Father. His words, His actions were all done under the direction and power of the Father. Jesus emphasized this when He said:

"Believest thou not that I am in the Father, and the Father in me? the words that I speak unto you I speak not of myself: but the Father that dwelleth in me, he doeth the works" (John 14:10).

How did Jesus obtain such a close oneness with His Father? It was through the baptism of the Holy Spirit and through prayer. When Jesus was baptized with water, He prayed:

"Now when all the people were baptized, it came to pass, that Jesus also being baptized, and praying, the heaven was opened, and the Holy Ghost descended in a bodily shape like a dove upon him, and a voice came from heaven, which said, Thou art my beloved Son; in thee I am well pleased" (Luke 3:21, 22).

In answer to Christ's prayer the Holy Spirit descended upon Him and He received the baptism of the Holy Spirit. Immediately after this event, He was led by the Spirit to spend 40 days and nights, fasting and praying in the wilderness.

"And Jesus being full of the Holy Ghost returned from Jordan, and was led by the Spirit into the wilderness, being forty days tempted of the devil. And in those days he did eat nothing: and when they were ended, he afterward hungered" (Luke 4:1, 2).

From this special communion with His Father, Christ came forth prepared to do the work He came to earth to do. He was empowered to be victorious over Satan and to defeat him:

"And Jesus returned in the power of the Spirit into Galilee: and there went out a fame of him through all the region round about" (verse 14).

The 40 days of prayer you have chosen to participate in is designed to do the same for you. During these 40 days you will experience empowerment to be victorious over Satan and to be a channel for Christ to minister through you to others.

Personal Reflection and Discussion

How will the Holy Spirit affect our prayer life?

In general, what do Christians tend to depend on more than prayer?

What kind of prayer life did Jesus have?

Because of Jesus' Spirit-baptism experience and prayer life, how did Jesus describe His relationship with His Father?

What did Jesus' Spirit-baptism experience and prayer life enable Him to do?

What kind of prayer life do you think Jesus wants you to have?

Prayer Activity

Call your prayer partner and discuss this devotional with him/her.
Pray with your prayer partner:

- **for God to continue to baptize each of you with His Holy Spirit.**
- **for God to give you a greater desire to pray.**
- **for the individuals on your prayer list.**

INCLUDE THE FOLLOWING BIBLE VERSE IN YOUR PRAYER:
"If my people, which are called by my name, shall humble themselves, and pray, and seek my face, and turn from their wicked ways; then will I hear from heaven, and will forgive their sin, and will heal their land" (2 Chron. 7:14).

Lead us into humility.
Put in our hearts a desire to be a praying people
and to turn from our wicked ways.
Hear our prayer, forgive us, and heal us of our backsliding.

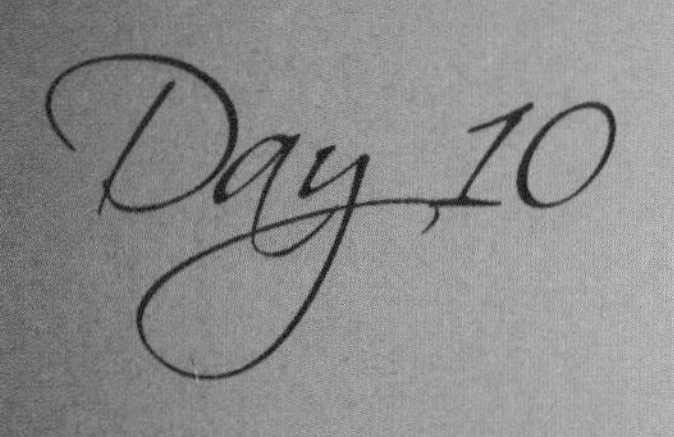

Jesus' and the Disciples' Example of Prayer

Time and again, we see Christ in prayer during His ministry on earth. After teaching great multitudes and healing them of their infirmities, we are told:

"And he withdrew himself into the wilderness, and prayed" (Luke 5:16).

Luke reports that before calling the 12 disciples:

"It came to pass in those days, that he went out into a mountain to pray, and continued all night in prayer to God. And when it was day, he called unto him his disciples: and of them he chose twelve, whom also he named apostles" (Luke 6:12, 13).

On the mount of transfiguration, Jesus prayed (Luke 9:29). He was drawn by the Spirit to be much with His heavenly Father in prayer. He responded to the deep, inner need for prayer that He felt. He knew it was only through such times of prayer that He would be one with the Father and be empowered to do the work He came to do.

Jesus gained His victories over Satan's works through times in prayer with the Father. When we read of Christ confronting Satan in the lives of men and women and nature in the forms of devil possession, disease, death, storm, etc., we do not see Christ at that moment in deep prayer with His Father, praying for the power to deliver. He had already received that power from the Father during the times of intimate prayer seasons. When confronted with Satan and his works, Jesus simply spoke the Word in the power and authority of the Father, and Satan's power was broken. Christ's word cast out devils, healed the sick, raised the dead, and quelled the storm.

The lesson is clear. Christ maintained His oneness with the Father and received His power over the enemy during His seasons of prayer with the Father. He then came away from these prayer times taking the Father with Him. He was conscious of the Father's presence moment by moment and day by day. Christ maintained this conscious and very real oneness with the Father throughout His life. Whenever He was confronted with Satan, He was prepared to meet the challenge and gain the victory because of His prayer life.

The example of Christ's prayer life was not lost on the disciples. Prayer was a central part of their ministry. When the growth of the church began to demand more and more of the disciples' time, deacons were established to "wait on tables." The disciples said of their priorities:

"But we will give ourselves *continually* to prayer, and to the ministry of the word" (Acts 6:4).

The early church members were men and women of prayer. It is recorded of them:

"And they continued stedfastly in the apostles' doctrine and fellowship, and in breaking of bread, and in prayers" (Acts 2:42).

These early believers prayed in the Temple, in their homes, and outside in nature.

"And on the sabbath we went out of the city by a river side, where prayer was wont to be made" (Acts 16:13).

All the apostles were men of prayer. Paul said he prayed day and night for the believers:

"Night and day praying exceedingly that we might see your face, and might perfect that which is lacking in your faith?" (1 Thess. 3:10).

Because the apostles were men of prayer, they were men of power in the Lord. The early Christians also were men and women of prayer, and God was able to do mighty wonders and miracles through them. Because of prayer the gospel went to the world.

"If ye continue in the faith grounded and settled, and be not moved away from the hope of the gospel, which ye have heard, and which was preached to every creature which is under heaven; whereof I, Paul am made a minister" (Col. 1:23).

God calls every Christian to become a mighty prayer warrior.

Personal Reflection and Discussion

Why did Jesus spend so much time in prayer?

How did Jesus' example in prayer affect the disciples?

What kind of prayer life did the early church members have?

How do you want your prayer life to change?

Prayer Activity

Call your prayer partner and discuss this devotional with him/her.
Pray with your prayer partner:

- **for God to continue to baptize each of you with His Holy Spirit.**
- **for God to lead you to become a prayer warrior as were Jesus and the disciples.**
- **for the individuals on your prayer list.**

INCLUDE THE FOLLOWING BIBLE VERSE IN YOUR PRAYER:
"Let me understand the teaching of your precepts; then I will meditate on your wonders" (Ps. 119:27, NIV).

Open my understanding to Your teachings.
Cause me to meditate constantly on You.

Day 11

Why is Prayer Necessary?

Even though most Christians believe prayer is important, many don't understand why prayer is really necessary. Many question If God is sovereign and able to carry out His will, why do we need to pray for Him to do what He already wants and plans to do anyway? Some reason that prayer is primarily for our benefit, but God is still going to do what He wants, whether we pray or not. The idea is popular that it's a "privilege" to pray but not really a necessity for God to carry out His will on earth. The truth of the matter is that it is necessary for God's children to pray. Why else would Jesus tell us to pray that God's will be done?

"After this manner therefore pray ye: Our Father which art in heaven, Hallowed be thy name. Thy kingdom come, Thy will be done in earth, as it is in heaven" (Matt. 6:9, 10).

If believers do not pray, God's desires will not be carried out in this earth.

Genesis records the Creation of this world and humankind:

"And God said, Let us make man in our image, after our likeness: and let them have dominion over the fish of the sea, and over the fowl of the air, and over the cattle, and over all the earth, and over every creeping thing that creepeth upon the earth. So God created man in his own image, in the image of God created he him; male and female created he them" (Gen. 1:26, 27).

The Hebrew words translated *likeness* and image indicate that God created humans in many ways like Himself.

God did something else when He created man. We are told in the above verse that God gave man "dominion" over this world. The Hebrew word translated *dominion* means "to rule," or "reign," over. As God's representative, Adam was to be the ruler of this world:

"And the Lord God took the man, and put him into the garden of Eden to dress it and to keep it" (Gen. 2:15).

Adam's responsibility to "keep" the earth meant he was to protect it from anything that would do harm. Adam was to be God's authoritative representative on earth. He was to be the earth's watchman, or guardian.

The psalmist further describes the position God gave man at Creation:

"For thou hast made him a little lower than the angels, and hast crowned him with glory and honour" (Ps. 8:5).

Looking again at the original Hebrew words translated *glory* and *honor,* we find that man was given authority similar to that of a king's reigning authority. Hence, we see that at Creation the earth was put under Adam's authority. What happened on earth depended on Adam.

Prayer is necessary, because from the beginning God intended to work *through* humans, not independent of them, in carrying out His will on earth. God works through the prayers of His people. When God wills to do something on this earth, it is necessary for humankind to pray that God will do it. Many examples of this are found in both the Old and New Testaments. We are to ask that God's "will be done in earth" (Matt. 6:10). We are to ask God to "give us this day our daily bread" (verse 11).

As Jesus saw the great need of the multitudes, He asked His disciples to make the following request to the Father:

"But when he saw the multitudes, he was moved with compassion on them, because they fainted, and were scattered abroad, as sheep having no shepherd. Then saith he unto his disciples, The harvest truly is plenteous, but the labourers are few; pray ye therefore the Lord of the harvest, that he will send forth labourers into his harvest" (Matt. 9:36-38).

God wants to send forth laborers into the harvest fields of this earth. However, it is necessary for the Christian to ask Him to do this.

Paul asked believers to pray for the advancement of the gospel:

"Finally, brethren, pray for us, that the word of the Lord may have free course, and be glorified, even as it is with you" (2 Thess. 3:1).

All of the things listed above are God's will; but it's necessary for man to pray for them because prayer releases God's power to carry out His will on this earth. Remember, it is God's plan to work *through* humankind, not work independent of us. Your prayers are essential for God's will to be done in your life and in the lives of those for whom you pray.

Personal Reflection and Discussion

Since God is "God," and has the power to do whatever He wants, isn't He going to carry out His will, whether we pray or not? Why, or why not?

____

____

What responsibility did Adam have when it came to God's will being done on earth?

____

____

When God wants to do something on earth, what is it necessary for the Christian to do?

____

____

Is prayer a necessity, or is it just a privilege?

____

How do you think Satan feels about your prayer time with God?

____

____

Prayer Activity

Call your prayer partner and discuss this devotional with him/her.
Pray with your prayer partner:

- **for God to continue to baptize each of you with His Holy Spirit.**
- **for God to give you a clear understanding of the necessity of prayer.**
- **for the individuals on your prayer list.**

INCLUDE THE FOLLOWING BIBLE VERSE IN YOUR PRAYER:
"Keep me from deceitful ways; be gracious to me through your law" (Ps. 119:29, NIV).

Turn me from my sinful ways.
Show favor on me that Your name may be glorified.

Day 12

Praying in the Spirit

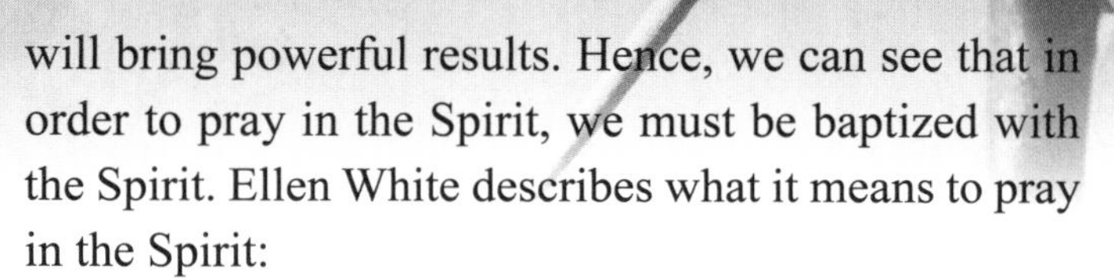

Every Christian is involved in warfare with the enemy with eternal consequences at stake. This battle is as real as any ever fought on this earth between nations. The battle is between the kingdom of God and the kingdom of darkness. Paul describes this battle as a wrestling match, which is up close and personal:

"For we wrestle not against flesh and blood, but against principalities, against powers, against the rulers of the darkness of this world, against spiritual wickedness in high places" (Eph. 6:12).

Paul next describes the armor of God that the Christian must put on for victory. Paul concludes his description of this warfare and our defense/offense against the enemy with the words: "Praying always with all prayer and supplication in the Spirit, and watching thereunto with all perseverance and supplication for all saints" (verse 18).

Note that Paul commands us to pray "always." We must become a prevailing prayer intercessor, praying consistently and persistently. Then he adds, "in the Spirit." Here we see that if we want victory over the enemy, praying in the Spirit is just as important as putting on the whole armor of God.

An important question, then, is What does it mean to pray in the Spirit? A brief definition would be that we pray in the Spirit when our prayers are prompted by the Holy Spirit. We are to be directed by the Spirit as to when to pray and what to pray for. The Holy Spirit is to guide us in every aspect of our prayer life. When we are praying in the Spirit, our prayers will be empowered by the Spirit. Our prayers will be effective and will bring powerful results. Hence, we can see that in order to pray in the Spirit, we must be baptized with the Spirit. Ellen White describes what it means to pray in the Spirit:

"By the Spirit every sincere prayer is indited [made up or composed], and such prayer is acceptable to God" (*The Desire of Ages,* p. 189).

Referring to Paul's statement in Romans 8:26 and 27, she writes:

"We must not only pray in Christ's name but by the inspiration of the Holy Spirit. This explains what is meant when it is said that the Spirit 'maketh intercession for us, with groanings which cannot be uttered.' Rom. 8:26. Such prayer God delights to answer" (*Christ's Object Lessons,* p. 147).

It is the Holy Spirit that calls us to prayer. He will show us some great need to pray for because God wants to begin acting in meeting that need. We read of such an experience in the case of Jesus praying for Peter:

"And the Lord said, Simon, Simon, behold, Satan hath desired to have you, that he may sift you as wheat: but I have prayed for thee, that thy faith fail not" (Luke 22:31, 32).

The Holy Spirit convicted Christ to pray for Peter—and even revealed what Satan's plan was concerning Peter. Once Christ knew this, He began praying for Peter. The Holy Spirit will do the same through us; He will bring to our mind someone to pray for. He may, or may not, reveal why He wants us to pray for them. The important thing is that we respond to the Spirit's prompting to pray.

Personal Reflection and Discussion

In Paul's description of the spiritual warfare in which we are engaged with Satan, what did he say about prayer?

____

____

How did Ellen White describe what it means to pray in the Spirit?

____

____

____

Describe a time when the Holy Spirit convicted you to pray for someone?

____

____

Do you desire to be a Christian who prays in the Spirit?

____

Prayer Activity

Call your prayer partner and discuss this devotional with him/her.
Pray with your prayer partner:

- **for God to continue to baptize each of you with His Holy Spirit.**
- **for God to direct your prayers by the Holy Spirit.**
- **for the individuals on your prayer list.**

INCLUDE THE FOLLOWING BIBLE VERSE IN YOUR PRAYER:
"O satisfy us early with thy mercy; that we may rejoice and be glad all our days" (Ps. 90:14).

Let us taste of Your mercy—lead us to confess our sins.
Bring us to rejoice fully in You.

Day 13

United Prayer in the Spirit

Christians uniting in prayer for a specific purpose has long been understood by believers to be an essential part of the Christian life. At one time I thought united prayer referred to two or more Christians coming together to pray. During prayer each one would pray for whatever came to their mind. Each prayer would have some common elements and would also have a number of requests that varied from those of the others who were praying. This is not the biblical definition for Christians uniting together for prayer. No, united prayer is two or more Christians praying for the same thing. They are united in desire, purpose, and request. They pray together at the same place and time with one prayer focus. If they cannot meet at the same place to pray, then they will pray at the same time with one prayer focus, or they may pray together on the phone. However, if possible, it is more strengthening to each if they actually meet together for prayer.

In our personal lives united prayer with fellow believers is a powerful force against Satan. This is why James counsels us to join together when praying for the sick and to pray for one another:

"Is any sick among you? let him call for the elders of the church; and let them pray over him, anointing him with oil in the name of the Lord: and the prayer of faith shall save the sick, and the Lord shall raise him up; and if he have committed sins, they shall be forgiven him. Confess your faults one to another, and pray one for another, that ye may be healed. The effectual fervent prayer of a righteous man availeth much" (James 5:14-16).

In fact, it is necessary for those ready to meet Jesus when He returns to have entered into genuine, united prayer for one another. We were not created to stand alone in our battle with Satan. We need one another's prayers for the complete victory over the enemy.

United prayer is also essential for the advancement of God's kingdom on this earth. Satan will resist every forward movement of God's work. United prayer will significantly increase God's power to advance His kingdom.

The Old Testament has numerous references to believers uniting together in prayer. The "teacher" in Ecclesiastes offers a significant lesson on the importance of others joining with us in our battle against our enemy, Satan:

"Though one may be overpowered, two can defend themselves. A cord of three strands is not quickly broken" (Eccl. 4:12, NIV).

Leviticus tells us:

"And five of you shall chase an hundred, and an hundred of you shall put ten thousand to flight: and your enemies shall fall before you by the sword" (Lev. 26:8).

If we try to stand alone in the battle against Satan and his temptations, we will be more easily overcome. As the "teacher" says, one alone may be more easily overpowered, while two can defend themselves—and three are even stronger. This is why fellowshipping in prayer with other Christians is so important and powerful.

Jesus uttered a most significant statement about the importance—and even necessity—of two or more believers joining together in fellowship and prayer.

"Again, I tell you that if two of you on earth agree about anything you ask for, it will be done for you by my Father in heaven. For where two or three come together in my name, there am I with them" (Matt. 18:19, 20, NIV).

When two or more believers pray in the Spirit, they can be confident that God will hear and answer their prayer:

"And this is the confidence that we have in him, that, if we ask any thing according to his will, he heareth us: and if we know that he hear us, whatsoever we ask, we know that we have the petitions that we desired of him" (1 John 5:14, 15).

Personal Reflection and Discussion

Describe united prayer in the Spirit.

___

___

Give a scripture that indicates that united prayer is even more effective than one Christian praying alone.

___

___

Do you think Satan wants Christians to unite together for prayer?

___

What can you do to become more involved in uniting in prayer with fellow believers?

___

___

Prayer Activity

Call your prayer partner and discuss this devotional with him/her.

Pray with your prayer partner:

- **for God to continue to baptize each of you with His Holy Spirit.**
- **for God to lead you to unite more often with fellow believers in prayer.**
- **for the individuals on your prayer list.**

INCLUDE THE FOLLOWING BIBLE VERSE IN YOUR PRAYER:
"Turn my eyes away from worthless things; preserve my life according to your word" (Ps. 119:37, NIV).

Cause me not to desire the things of this earth.
Restore my spiritual life.

Day 14

Persevering Prayer in the Spirit

Throughout the centuries persevering prayer has been considered an essential part of the advancement of God's kingdom on earth. However, those of us who live in the Western culture tend to want quick answers to our problems. Many times this quick-fix attitude finds its way into our prayer life. Often we will pray for something occasionally, but not perseveringly. The truth is that persevering prayer is not an option; it is a necessity, just as united prayer is a necessity, if we are to be victorious over our adversary personally and corporately as a church. Those ready to meet Jesus will know from personal experience what it means to persevere in prayer. Prayer will have played a major role in preparing them for that great event.

Jesus was personally acquainted with the necessity for persevering prayer. Many times He spent entire nights in prayer. In Luke 18, He related a story that clearly illustrated the necessity for every believer to enter into persevering prayer. Two key phrases make His point. Luke introduces the parable with the words:

"And He spake a parable unto them to this end, that men ought always to pray, and not to faint" (Luke 18:1).

The purpose of this parable was to teach us of the *necessity* of persevering in prayer. Luke knew Jesus taught that we *ought,* or *should* (NIV), *always* pray and not faint, or stop praying, until we get the answer. The Greek form of the verb pray is continuous action. Jesus is teaching in this parable that we should keep on praying, and not stop or give up.

The second phrase that reinforces the importance of persevering prayer is this:

"And shall not God avenge his own elect, which cry day and night unto him, though he bear long with them?" (verse 7).

Here Jesus clearly teaches that many times God's answers to our prayers will come only as the result of our crying to him "day and night." Quick praying will not bring the results that consistent, persevering prayer will.

Ellen White sensed the spiritual weakness among God's people in her day. She asked God's angel why this was the case. Note the answer:

"I asked the angel why there was no more faith and power in Israel. He said: 'Ye let go of the arm of the Lord too soon. Press your petitions to the throne, and hold on by strong faith. The promises are sure. Believe ye receive the things ye ask for, and ye shall have them.' I was then pointed to Elijah. He was subject to like passions as we are, and he prayed earnestly. His faith endured the trial. Seven times he prayed before the Lord, and at last the cloud was seen" (*Early Writings,* p. 73).

Many of us still "let go of the arm of the Lord too soon." We must come to learn how to prevail long with the Lord in prayer.

Personal Reflection and Discussion

What does it mean to persevere with God in prayer?

____

____

Do you think persevering prayer is easy for the average Christian in the Western world? Why, or why not?

____

____

What did Jesus say about the importance of persevering prayer?

____

____

What did the angel tell Ellen White concerning the reason there was so little power in God's church today?

____

____

Prayer Activity

Call your prayer partner and discuss this devotional with him/her.
Pray with your prayer partner:

- **for God to continue to baptize each of you with His Holy Spirit.**
- **for God to lead you to learn how to persevere in prayer.**
- **for the individuals on your prayer list.**

INCLUDE THE FOLLOWING BIBLE VERSE IN YOUR PRAYER:
"As the bridegroom rejoiceth over the bride, so shall thy God rejoice over thee. I have set watchmen upon thy walls, O Jerusalem, which shall never hold their peace day nor night; ye that make mention of the Lord, keep not silence, and give him no rest, till he establish, and till he make Jerusalem a praise in the earth" (Isa. 62:5-7).

Cause us to pray to You constantly until You revive us, and make us a praise to Your name in this community.

Day 15

Intercessory Prayer in the Spirit for Others

The principle of persevering prayer applies to every area of the Christian's life, including our efforts to lead others to Christ. It should be clear from our previous discussion that our prayers are necessary for the salvation of those in our circle of family and friends.

Paul exhorts the Christian to make "intercession" for all men:

"I exhort therefore, that, first of all, supplications, prayers, intercessions, and giving of thanks, be made for all men; For kings, and for all that are in authority; that we may lead a quiet and peaceable life in all godliness and honesty. For this is good and acceptable in the sight of God our Saviour" (1Tim. 2:1-3).

We are to bring about meetings with God through intercessory prayer. Our prayers for the lost bring about meetings of reconciliation between them and God and meetings of dissolution between them and Satan. Intercessory prayer is a major element in the . . . "ministry of reconciliation" . . . every Christian is called to participate in:

"And all things are of God, who hath reconciled us to himself by Jesus Christ, and hath given to us the ministry of reconciliation; to wit, that God was in Christ, reconciling the world unto himself, not imputing their trespasses unto them; and hath committed unto us the word of reconciliation" (2 Cor. 5:18, 19).

In His prayer to the Father in John 17, Christ is praying an intercessory prayer that "oneness," or "unity," take place between the Father and the believers:

"Neither pray I for these alone, but for them also which shall believe on me through their word; That they all may be one; as thou, Father, art in me, and I in thee, that they also may be one in us: that the world may believe that thou hast sent me" (John 17:20, 21).

Christ is praying for complete reconciliation between the Father and all believers. He not only prayed that intercessory prayer for us 2,000 years ago, He continues to pray an intercessory prayer for us today:

"Wherefore he is able also to save them to the uttermost that come unto God by him, seeing he ever liveth to make intercession for them" (Heb. 7:25).

Throughout the letters of Paul we read of his continual intercession to God on behalf of those to whom he is writing:

"For God is my witness, whom I serve with my spirit in the gospel of his Son, that without ceasing I make mention of you always in my prayers" (Rom. 1:9).

"Wherefore I also, after I heard of your faith in the Lord Jesus, and love unto all the saints, cease not to give thanks for you, making mention of you in my prayers" (Eph. 1:15, 16).

"For this cause we also, since the day we heard it, do not cease to pray for you, and to desire that ye might be filled with the knowledge of his will in all wisdom and spiritual understanding" (Col. 1:9).

Paul knew them well and loved them deeply. He certainly understood the necessity of continually making intercession for all the saints. He encourages every Christian to do the same for one another:

"Praying always with all prayer and supplication in the Spirit, and watching thereunto with all perseverance and supplication for all saints" (Eph. 6:18).

God revealed the necessity of intercessory prayer when Samuel spoke the following words to King Saul:

"God forbid that I should sin against the Lord in ceasing to pray for you" (1 Sam. 12:23).

Here we learn that it is actually a sin for us to refuse to pray for one another. Ellen White encouraged prayer for one another with these words:

"Although God dwells not in temples made with hands, yet he honors with his presence the assemblies of his people. He has promised that when they come together to seek him, to acknowledge their sins, and to *pray for one another,* he will meet with them by his Spirit. But those who assemble to worship him should put away every evil thing. Unless they can worship him in spirit and truth and in the beauty of holiness, their coming together will be of no avail" (*Review and Herald,* November 30, 1905).

As Christians are daily filled with the Spirit, God will lead in their intercessory prayer life. He will bring to their mind whom to pray for and, often, what to pray for in each person's life. Hence, we can clearly see why Satan will do everything in his power to make us believe that it is not essential or important that we specifically pray for one another. He wants us to believe that it is not really necessary for us to pray for those who are out of Christ. He wants us to believe that God will work for the salvation of the lost even if we don't specifically pray for those in our circle of family and friends. Hopefully, you will not believe his lies about the unimportance of prayer for others or yourself. This is why he will attack our prayer life, perhaps more than any other aspect of our spiritual life.

Personal Reflection and Discussion

When the Christian intercedes in prayer for someone, what is he/she actually doing?

___

___

For what, specifically, did Jesus intercede in prayer when He prayed for His followers, as recorded in John 17?

___

___

Is intercessory prayer a privilege or a necessity? Why?

___

How has Satan attacked your prayer life?

___

___

How can you become a more effective prayer intercessor for others?

___

Prayer Activity

Call your prayer partner and discuss this devotional with him/her.

Pray with your prayer partner:

- **for God to continue to baptize each of you with His Holy Spirit.**
- **for God to lead you to become an effective prayer intercessor for others.**
- **for the individuals on your prayer list.**

INCLUDE THE FOLLOWING BIBLE VERSE IN YOUR PRAYER:

"Then will I sprinkle clean water upon you, and ye shall be clean: from all your filthiness, and from all your idols, will I cleanse you. A new heart also will I give you, and a new spirit will I put within you: and I will take away the stony heart out of your flesh, and I will give you an heart of flesh. And I will put my spirit within you, and cause you to walk in my statutes, and ye shall keep my judgments, and do them" (Eze. 36:25-27).

Open our eyes to the worldly idols in our lives and cleanse us from them.
Give us new hearts and a desire to serve You
—cause us to obey You in all our ways.

Day 16

Praying God's Promises in the Spirit

God has given us many promises in the Bible to meet our every need. Both the Old and New Testaments have outstanding examples of God's people claiming the promises of His Word when facing difficulties.

One of my first exposures to the Bible teachings on prayer was in *The ABC's of Bible Prayer,* a book by Glen Coon. I learned the concept of claiming God's promises in prayer as a young Christian, and it has proved to be a great blessing throughout my life and ministry. The prayer formula is simple:

Ask:

"Ask, and it shall be given you; seek, and ye shall find; knock, and it shall be opened unto you" (Matt. 7:7).

Believe:

"Therefore I say unto you, what things soever ye desire, when ye pray, believe that ye receive them, and ye shall have them" (Mark 11:24).

Claim the promise with thanksgiving before any answer is seen:

"Then they took away the stone from the place where the dead was laid. And Jesus lifted up his eyes, and said, Father, I thank thee that thou hast heard me. And I knew that thou hearest me always: but because of the people which stand by I said it, that they may believe that thou hast sent me. And when he thus had spoken, he cried with a loud voice, Lazarus, come forth" (John 11:41-43).

In these verses we see that Jesus thanked the Father for hearing and answering His prayer before there was evidence of it being answered.

God's promises are sure. We can be confident that God will do what He says:

"God is not a man, that he should lie; neither the son of man, that he should repent: hath he said, and shall he not do it? or hath he spoken, and shall he not make it good?" (Num. 23:19).

And He can do what He promises:

"Ah Lord God! behold, thou hast made the heaven and the earth by thy great power and stretched out arm, and there is nothing too hard for thee" (Jer. 32:17).

Just as the oak tree is in the acorn, so is the fulfillment of God's promise in the promise itself when claimed by faith. Concerning the promises of God's Word, Ellen White writes:

"In every command and in every promise of the word of God is the power, the very life of God, by which the command may be fulfilled and the promise realized" (*Christ's Object Lessons,* p. 38).

God's power and very life is contained in the promises of the Bible. Nothing can stand in the way of His promises being fulfilled when we claim them by faith in persevering prayer.

In 2 Chronicles 20 we find a marvelous prayer model of claiming God's promises. Jehoshaphat, King of Judah, was facing an imminent invasion by a confederacy of armies. He had made preparation for such a crisis by building up Judah's army and defenses. He had more than 1 million well-trained men ready for battle. However, when the threat became known to the king, his first response was not to look to his preparations for war, but rather look to the Lord.

When we face problems in life our response should be the same—look to the Lord first. This doesn't mean that we don't do what we can to meet whatever situation may arise. The danger is that we have the tendency to go immediately to our human resources for help and deliverance. Our mind often begins formulating ways to solve the problem rather than turning to God first. Jehoshaphat's response is a good example for us to follow.

Jehoshaphat's prayer is recorded in 2 Chronicles 20:6-13:

"And said, O Lord God of our fathers, art not thou God in heaven? and rulest not thou over all the kingdoms of the heathen? and in thine hand is there not power and might, so that none is able to withstand thee? Art not thou our God, who didst drive out the inhabitants of this land before thy people Israel, and gavest it to the seed of Abraham thy friend for ever? And they dwelt therein, and have built thee a sanctuary therein for thy name, saying, If, when evil cometh upon us, as the sword, judgment, or pestilence, or famine, we stand before this house, and in thy presence, (for thy name is in this house,) and cry unto thee in our affliction, then thou wilt hear and help. And now, behold, the children of Ammon and Moab and mount Seir, whom thou wouldest not let Israel invade, when they came out of the land of Egypt, but they turned from them, and destroyed them not; behold, I say, how they reward us, to come to cast us out of thy possession, which thou hast given us to inherit. O our God, wilt thou not judge them? for we have no might against this great company that cometh against us; neither know we what to do: but our eyes are upon thee. And all Judah stood before the Lord, with their little ones, their wives, and their children."

This prayer reveals five steps for victoriously praying for the promises of God:

- First, the king began by *praising* God's attributes, especially those related to the problem he was facing (verse 6). When facing an attacking enemy, as Jehoshaphat was, it was encouraging for him to recall that God rules over all the kingdoms of the nations, that "power and might" are in His hand, and that no one can withstand Him.
- Second, the king recalled *past victories,* similar to the present victory Judah needed (verse 7). Recalling God's provision in the past, as related to our present need, reminds us of God's faithfulness and builds our faith.
- Third, he stated in prayer a promise God had made to His people in the past—a *promise* related to the problem he was facing (verses 8 and 9).
- After these three steps in prayer, Jehoshaphat then stated the *problem* (verses 10-12).
- Finally, he *praised* God before any evidence of victory was seen (verses 18 and 19).

Note the formula for praying God's promises—and not focusing on the problem: *praise, past victories, promise, problem, praise.*

Personal Reflection and Discussion

Relate a time when you prayed God's promise, and how that differed from a time you only focused on the problem in prayer?

____

____

What are the ABC's of prayer?

____

What are the elements of King Jehoshaphat's prayer?

____

____

What can you do to begin praying God's promises rather than the problem?

____

____

List your favorite promises in God's Word?

____

____

Prayer Activity

Call your prayer partner and discuss this devotional with him/her.

Pray with your prayer partner:

- **for God to continue to baptize each of you with His Holy Spirit.**
- **for God to lead you to learn how to pray His promises rather than focusing on the problems you face.**
- **for the individuals on your prayer list.**

INCLUDE THE FOLLOWING BIBLE VERSE IN YOUR PRAYER:
"Give me understanding, and I will keep your law and obey it with all my heart" (Ps. 119:34, NIV).

Give me the desire to obey You with all my heart.

Day 17

SECTION THREE

Spirit Baptism and Evangelism

Gospel Work Finished Under Holy Spirit Power

Jesus foretold that the "gospel of the kingdom shall be preached in all the world for a witness unto all nations; and then shall the end come" (Matt. 24:14). Just before Jesus comes, there will be a tremendous evangelism explosion that will produce a mighty witness of the gospel on this earth.

The prophet Joel foretold two great Holy Spirit outpourings—the former or early rain and latter rain:

"Be glad then, ye children of Zion, and rejoice in the Lord your God: for he hath given you the former rain moderately, and he will cause to come down for you the rain, the former rain, and the latter rain in the first month" (Joel 2:23).

Peter indicated in his sermon on the day of Pentecost that the former, or early, rain outpouring of the Holy Spirit had begun on that day:

"But this is that which was spoken by the prophet Joel; and it shall come to pass in the last days, saith God, I will pour out of my Spirit upon all flesh: and your sons and your daughters shall prophesy, and your young men shall see visions, and your old men shall dream dreams: And on my servants and on my handmaidens I will pour out in those days of my Spirit; and they shall prophesy" (Acts 2:16-18).

This early rain of the Spirit is also called the baptism of the Holy Spirit:

"And, being assembled together with them, commanded them that they should not depart from Jerusalem, but wait for the promise of the Father, which, saith he, ye have heard of me. For John truly baptized with water; but ye shall be baptized with the Holy Ghost not many days hence. . . . But ye shall receive power, after that the Holy Ghost is come upon you: and ye shall be witnesses unto me both in Jerusalem, and in all Judaea, and in Samaria, and unto the uttermost part of the earth" (Acts 1:4-8).

The book of Acts describes the great evangelism explosion that took place at that time. Thousands were won to Christ.

Every Christian who has read the book of Acts has probably longed for the day that a similar mighty working of the Holy Spirit will take place again. Several years ago I started to better understand how the mighty moving of God's Spirit will happen as I began studying and seeking the baptism of the Holy Spirit.

God began clarifying how "anointed, Spirit-filled" believers will be mightily used by Him to win thousands to Christ. I realized that the professional evangelist and radio or television broadcasts would not finish God's last-day work, though these will play a role. Rather, God's work will be finished when His people seek and experience the baptism of the Holy Spirit and allow Christ to reach out to others through them. God's work will not be finished by some new program or method; God will finish His work through Spirit-filled believers who surrender themselves completely to Christ and allow Him to live in them and minister to others through them. That is why Jesus told the disciples to wait for the baptism of the Holy Spirit before they sought to take the gospel to the world (Acts 1:4-8). Even though they had been with Jesus and ministered to others for three and one half years, they weren't yet ready to tell the world about Jesus. They needed to wait for the power of the Spirit.

When consecrated Christians experience Christ in this way, the second great evangelism explosion will take place, and the second great outpouring of the Holy Spirit, called the latter rain, will fall upon this earth. This section of these devotional studies is dedicated to helping the reader understand how this second great evangelism explosion will take place, and how every believer can be a part of it. In fact, all who are ready to meet Jesus when He returns will have had a part in it.

Personal Reflection and Discussion

Have you experienced the power of the Holy Spirit as much as you would like in witnessing to others?

What were the disciples to wait for before they took the gospel to the world, and why?

What do you think will be the major factor in God's work being finished?

Do you want to be part of the last great evangelism explosion?

How can you become part of this last evangelistic work of God?

Prayer Activity

Call your prayer partner and discuss this devotional with him/her.

Pray with your prayer partner:

- **for God to continue to baptize each of you with His Holy Spirit.**
- **for God to lead you to learn how you can become an effective witness for Jesus.**
- **for the individuals on your prayer list.**

INCLUDE THE FOLLOWING BIBLE VERSE IN YOUR PRAYER:
"Lord, I have heard of your fame; I stand in awe of your deeds, O Lord. Renew them in our day, in our time make them known; in wrath remember mercy" (Hab. 3:2).

Lead us from our sin; have mercy on us and forgive us.
Glorify Your name through great works of salvation.

Day 18

Spirit Baptism and Witnessing

Seventh-day Adventists, as well as many other Christians, have been predicting the second coming of Christ for many years. Seventh-day Adventists believe that Christ could have come before now if certain things would have happened. The parable of the 10 virgins teaches that the Bridegroom's return would be delayed.

What is at the heart of this delay in Christ's return? I believe there are two reasons. First, God's people are not ready. Second, the work of preaching the gospel to the world, warning them of Christ's coming, and events surrounding that event haven't happened. The three angels' messages of Revelation chapter 14 haven't gone to the world, as they must before Christ returns:

"And I saw another angel fly in the midst of heaven, having the everlasting gospel to preach unto them that dwell on the earth, and to every nation, and kindred, and tongue, and people, saying with a loud voice, Fear God, and give glory to him; for the hour of his judgment is come: and worship him that made heaven, and earth, and the sea, and the fountains of waters. And there followed another angel, saying, Babylon is fallen, is fallen, that great city, because she made all nations drink of the wine of the wrath of her fornication. And the third angel followed them, saying with a loud voice, If any man worship the beast and his image, and receive his mark in his forehead, or in his hand, the same shall drink of the wine of the wrath of God, which is poured out without mixture into the cup of his indignation; and he shall be tormented with fire and brimstone in the presence of the holy angels, and in the presence of the Lamb: And the smoke of their torment ascendeth up for ever and ever: and they have no rest day nor night, who worship the beast and his image, and whosoever receiveth the mark of his name. Here is the patience of the saints: here are they that keep the commandments of God, and the faith of Jesus. And I heard a voice from heaven saying unto me, Write, Blessed are the dead which die in the Lord from henceforth: Yea, saith the Spirit, that they may rest from their labours; and their works do follow them. And I looked, and behold a white cloud, and upon the cloud one sat like unto the Son of man, having on his head a golden crown, and in his hand a sharp sickle" (Rev. 14:6-14).

Great and terrible events are to come upon this earth just prior to Christ's second coming. In the past God's people have not been ready for such events, as in Noah's day when the flood didn't come until the warning of the flood had gone out to earth's inhabitants, and the boat was ready for the deluge:

"But as the days of Noe were, so shall also the coming of the Son of man be" (Matt. 24:37).

The warning message will be given and the "boat," or church, will be ready. Then the end will come.

How did Christ get the most serious message of Noah to the world of Noah's day? Peter tells us in his first letter. The Holy Spirit that "quickened" Christ, or raised Him from the grave, is the Spirit by which Christ "preached" through Noah to men and women (called spirits) who were captives, or prisoners, of Satan:

"For Christ also hath once suffered for sins, the just for the unjust, that he might bring us to God, being put to death in the flesh, but quickened by the Spirit: by which also he went and preached unto the spirits in prison; which sometime were disobedient, when once the longsuffering of God waited in the days of Noah, while the ark was a preparing, wherein few, that is, eight souls were saved by water" (1 Peter 3:18-20).

Numbers 27:15 and 16 indicates that the Bible uses the word *spirits* to refer to living men and women:

"And Moses spake unto the Lord, saying, Let the Lord, the God of the spirits of all flesh, set a man over the congregation."

The Bible also indicates that the term *prison,* or *prisoners,* can refer to men and women under Satan's power of sin and deception:

"I the Lord have called thee in righteousness, and will hold thine hand, and will keep thee, and give thee for a covenant of the people, for a light of the Gentiles; to open the blind eyes, to bring out the prisoners from the prison, and them that sit in darkness out of the prison house" (Isa. 42:6, 7).

Hence, we see from Scripture that it was Christ, by the Holy Spirit, speaking through Noah who prepared the inhabitants of the earth for the flood. So it will be in the last days just before Christ's second coming (Matt. 24:37). Christ will speak by the Holy Spirit through Spirit-filled Christians to prepare the world for the Second Advent.

I have been a Seventh-day Adventist Christian for many years, and a pastor for most of those years. In my denomination, as well as in many other Christian organizations, I believe much time and money has been spent on plans, programs, and methods to bring Christ to the world. I'm not against plans, programs, and methods, but I'm afraid that we have, more often than not, depended on these things to finish God's work. Plans, programs, and methods will not finish God's work. Great speakers, marvelous Christian musical concerts, or satellites will not finish God's work. *God's Holy Spirit will finish God's work*—God's Spirit, speaking and ministering through Spirit-filled men and women.

Personal Reflection and Discussion

Why do you think Jesus has not come yet?

____

____

What did Jesus say about Noah's day and our day?

____

____

How did God finish His warning work in Noah's day?

____

____

What, or whom, do you think God will use most in finishing His work on earth?

____

____

What can you do to become one whom God will use to finish His work?

____

____

Prayer Activity

Call your prayer partner and discuss this devotional with him/her.

Pray with your prayer partner:

- **for God to continue to baptize each of you with His Holy Spirit.**
- **for God to witness through you by His Spirit, as He did through Noah.**
- **for the individuals on your prayer list.**

INCLUDE THE FOLLOWING BIBLE VERSE IN YOUR PRAYER:
"Direct me in the path of your commands, for there I find delight" (Ps. 119:35, NIV).

Cause me to delight in Your commands and not in things of this world.

Day 19

The Necessity of Spirit Baptism in Witnessing

The truth of the necessity of the baptism of the Holy Spirit for witnessing is clearly revealed in the New Testament. We see it in the experience of Jesus. Luke describes Christ's water baptism in chapter three of his gospel. He tells us that at Christ's baptism He prayed, and the "Holy Spirit descended" upon Him:

"Now when all the people were baptized, it came to pass, that Jesus also being baptized, and praying, the heaven was opened, and the Holy Ghost descended in a bodily shape like a dove upon him, and a voice came from heaven, which said, Thou art my beloved Son; in thee I am well pleased" (Luke 3:21, 22).

From that time forward Luke says that Jesus was "filled" with the Holy Spirit and ministered in the "power" of the Spirit:

"And Jesus being full of the Holy Ghost returned from Jordan, and was led by the Spirit into the wilderness" (Luke 4:1). And Jesus returned in the power of the Spirit into Galilee: and there went out a fame of him through all the region round about" (verse 14).

Before this Spirit-infilling, or baptism, no ministry of Christ is recorded; we are told of no followers being drawn to Him. Immediately after being baptized, or filled with the Spirit, we are told that "there went out a fame of him through all the region round about." After Christ was filled with the Holy Spirit, we read throughout the gospels of thousands responding to His message and ministry. All of Christ's teachings were anointed by Holy Spirit power, which was the result of His being filled with the Holy Spirit, in answer to His prayer at the time of His water baptism:

"The Spirit of the Lord is upon me, because he hath anointed me to preach the gospel to the poor; he hath sent me to heal the brokenhearted, to preach deliverance to the captives, and recovering of sight to the blind, to set at liberty them that are bruised, to preach the acceptable year of the Lord" (verses 18, 19).

"Until the day in which he was taken up, after that he through the Holy Ghost had given commandments unto the apostles whom he had chosen" (Acts 1:2).

"How God anointed Jesus of Nazareth with the Holy Ghost and with power: who went about doing good, and healing all that were oppressed of the devil; for God was with him" (Acts 10:38).

Jesus well knew the importance and necessity of Spirit-filled ministry. This is why He told the disciples to wait for the promise of the baptism of the Holy Spirit before they went forth to proclaim the gospel.

"And, being assembled together with them, commanded them that they should not depart from Jerusalem, but wait for the promise of the Father, which, saith he, ye have heard of me. For John truly baptized with water; but ye shall be baptized with the Holy Ghost not many days hence" (Acts 1:4, 5).

Jesus went on to tell them that they would receive power to witness when they received the baptism of the Holy Spirit:

"But ye shall receive power, after that the Holy Ghost is come upon you: and ye shall be witnesses unto me both in Jerusalem, and in all Judaea, and in Samaria, and unto the uttermost part of the earth" (verse 8).

The disciples did what Jesus asked them to do. They waited and unitedly prayed for the promise of the baptism of the Holy Spirit to be fulfilled to them.

"These all continued with one accord in prayer and supplication, with the women, and Mary the mother of

Jesus, and with his brethren" (verse 14).

In answer to their 10 days of praying, the Holy Spirit came on the day of Pentecost and "they were all filled with the Holy Ghost:"

"And when the day of Pentecost was fully come, they were all with one accord in one place. And suddenly there came a sound from heaven as of a rushing mighty wind, and it filled all the house where they were sitting. And there appeared unto them cloven tongues like as of fire, and it sat upon each of them. And they were all filled with the Holy Ghost, and began to speak with other tongues, as the Spirit gave them utterance" (Acts 2:1-4).

What happened next reveals one of the main purposes for the baptism of the Holy Spirit. God used these Spirit-filled believers to tell of the "wonderful works of God":

"And they were all amazed and marvelled, saying one to another, Behold, are not all these which speak Galilaeans? And how hear we every man in our own tongue, wherein we were born? Parthians, and Medes, and Elamites, and the dwellers in Mesopotamia, and in Judaea, and Cappadocia, in Pontus, and Asia, Phrygia, and Pamphylia, in Egypt, and in the parts of Libya about Cyrene, and strangers of Rome, Jews and proselytes, Cretes and Arabians, we do hear them speak in our tongues the wonderful works of God" (verses 7-11).

God even surmounted language barriers to get the good news of a risen Savior to the Jews who were present on that day. Three thousand responded to Peter's Spirit empowered sermon:

"Then they that gladly received his word were baptized: and the same day there were added unto them about three thousand souls" (verse 41).

The early church continued to minister under the anointing power of the Holy Spirit. God marvelously worked through these Spirit-filled believers to win many others to Christ:

"Praising God, and having favour with all the people. And the Lord added to the church daily such as should be saved" (verse 47).

These early Christians recognized the urgency of receiving the baptism of the Holy Spirit in order to live a godly life and effectively witness for their Lord.

Spirit baptism was so important that when many Samaritan men and women had accepted Jesus as their Savior and were baptized in water under Philip's ministry, Peter and John were sent to meet with them. Soon after their arrival, they laid hands on these newly-baptized believers and prayed for them to receive the baptism of the Holy Spirit:

"But when they believed Philip preaching the things concerning the kingdom of God, and the name of Jesus Christ, they were baptized, both men and women. Then Simon himself believed also: and when he was baptized, he continued with Philip, and wondered, beholding the miracles and signs which were done. Now when the apostles which were at Jerusalem heard that Samaria had received the word of God, they sent unto them Peter and John: who, when they were come down, prayed for them, that they might receive the Holy Ghost: (For as yet he was fallen upon none of them: only they were baptized in the name of the Lord Jesus.) Then laid they their hands on them, and they received the Holy Ghost" (Acts 8:12-17).

We see the same priority in God's call to Saul on the road to Damascus. Christ revealed Himself to Saul in a vision:

"And Saul, yet breathing out threatenings and slaughter against the disciples of the Lord, went unto the high priest, and desired of him letters to Damascus to the synagogues, that if he found any of this way, whether they were men or women, he might bring them bound unto Jerusalem. And as he journeyed, he came near Damascus: and suddenly there shined round about him a light from heaven: and he fell to the earth, and heard a voice saying unto him, Saul, Saul, why persecutest thou me? And he said, Who art thou, Lord? And the Lord said, I am Jesus whom thou persecutest: it is hard for thee to kick against the pricks. And he trembling and astonished said, Lord, what wilt thou have me to do? And the Lord said unto him, Arise, and go into the city, and it shall be told thee what thou must do. And the men which journeyed with him stood speechless, hearing a voice, but seeing no man" (Acts 9:1-7).

Then Christ directed Saul to go to Damascus and wait for further instruction, after which God sent Ananias to Saul to lay hands on him and pray for the baptism of the Holy Spirit and healing of his eyesight:

"And Ananias went his way, and entered into the house; and putting his hands on him said, Brother Saul, the Lord, even Jesus, that appeared unto thee in the way as thou camest, hath sent me, that thou mightest receive thy sight, and be filled with the Holy Ghost. And immediately there fell from his eyes as it had been scales: and he received sight forthwith, and arose, and was baptized" (verses 17, 18).

As a result of the Spirit's infilling, "Saul increased the more in strength" (verse 22). The word strength is not simply referring to physical strength. The context indicates that Saul increased in spiritual strength and power in proclaiming the gospel. This spiritual strength and power for witnessing resulted from the baptism of the Holy Spirit he had received when Ananias prayed for him.

Personal Reflection and Discussion

When did Jesus' service for His Father become powerful, and how does the Bible describe His Spirit-baptized ministry?

What did Jesus tell the disciples to do before they began ministering?

What results did the early church have after they received the baptism of the Holy Spirit?

Why did God send Peter and John to the new Samaritan believers, and Ananias to Saul after his conversion?

Prayer Activity

Call your prayer partner and discuss this devotional with him/her.
Pray with your prayer partner:

- **for God to continue to baptize each of you with His Holy Spirit.**
- **for God to witness through you in the power of the Spirit.**
- **for the individuals on your prayer list.**

INCLUDE THE FOLLOWING BIBLE VERSE IN YOUR PRAYER:
"I am laid low in the dust; preserve my life according to your word" (Ps. 119:25, NIV).

We are far from where we should be spiritually.
Restore us spiritually as You have promised.

Day 20

Spirit Baptism and Preparing the Way for Christ's Advent

The prophet Malachi foretold that God would send Elijah, referring to an "Elijah message," just prior to the coming of Jesus Christ:

"Behold, I will send you Elijah the prophet before the coming of the great and dreadful day of the Lord" (Mal. 4:5).

This prophecy has two applications. One applies to Christ's first advent; the other applies to His second coming.

The gospel writer, Luke, tells us that John the Baptist fulfilled the first application of this prophecy of Malachi:

"And he shall go before him in the spirit and power of Elias, to turn the hearts of the fathers to the children, and the disobedient to the wisdom of the just; to make ready a people prepared for the Lord" (Luke 1:17).

John the Baptist went forward in ministry in the "spirit and power" of Elijah. To what did this refer? It meant that he was Spirit-filled and preached a Spirit-anointed message to prepare the people of his day for the Messiah, who would soon appear:

"For he shall be great in the sight of the Lord, and shall drink neither wine nor strong drink; and he shall be filled with the Holy Ghost, even from his mother's womb" (Luke 1:15).

The power of the Holy Spirit attended John's preaching. Multitudes came to hear him, and many were baptized:

"In those days came John the Baptist, preaching in the wilderness of Judaea, and saying, Repent ye: for the kingdom of heaven is at hand. For this is he that was spoken of by the prophet Esaias, saying, The voice of one crying in the wilderness, prepare ye the way of the Lord, make his paths straight. And the same John had his raiment of camel's hair, and a leathern girdle about his loins; and his meat was locusts and wild honey. Then went out to him Jerusalem, and all Judaea, and all the region round about Jordan, and were baptized of him in Jordan, confessing their sins" (Matt. 3:1-6).

Jesus was well aware of Malachi's prophecy, and He applied it to the mission and message of John the Baptist:

"For all the prophets and the law prophesied until John. And if ye will receive it, this is Elias, which was for to come. He that hath ears to hear, let him hear (Matt. 11:13-15).

Malachi's prophecy has a second application, referring to a people who will give a serious warning message just before Jesus comes, which is called the three angels' messages:

"And I saw another angel fly in the midst of heaven, having the everlasting gospel to preach unto them that dwell on the earth, and to every nation, and kindred, and tongue, and people, saying with a loud voice, Fear God, and give glory to him; for the hour of his judgment is come: and worship him that made heaven, and earth, and the sea, and the fountains of waters. And there followed another angel, saying, Babylon is fallen, is fallen, that great city, because she made all nations drink of the wine of the wrath of her fornication. And the third angel followed them, saying with a loud voice, If any man worship the beast and his image, and receive his mark in his forehead, or in his hand, the same shall drink of the wine of the wrath of God, which is poured out without mixture into the cup of his indignation; and he shall be tormented with fire and brimstone in the presence of the holy angels, and in the presence of the Lamb: And the smoke of their torment ascendeth up for ever and ever: and they have no rest day nor night, who worship the beast and his image, and whosoever receiveth the mark of his name. Here is the patience of the saints: here are they that keep the commandments of God, and the faith of Jesus" (Rev. 14:6-12).

This last-day Elijah message is intended to prepare men and women for Christ's second coming. As John the Baptist had to be Spirit-filled to give the Elijah message of his day, so God's last-day believers must be Spirit-filled to give the last-day Elijah message to the world today. This last-day message of warning that will be given by a Spirit-filled people will go forth in the "spirit and power" of Elijah, as did John's message.

Why hasn't this final message yet been given with such power? It has been preached for more than 150 years. Millions of dollars have been, and are being, spent to give it. What's wrong? I personally believe our lack of understanding and experiencing the baptism of the Holy Spirit is the answer. I don't mean that God has not blessed our efforts to warn the world of Christ's second coming and the issues involved in these last days. I am saying that we have not yet tapped into the mighty blessing and power that awaits us when God's people become a Spirit-filled people. When that happens the last-day message of Elijah will go forth in the "spirit and power" of Elijah.

Personal Reflection and Discussion

What are the two applications of Malachi's prophecy about Elijah?

____

How was the first application of Malachi's prophecy fulfilled?

____

What did John the Baptist have that enabled him to give the Elijah message in his day?

____

What is the Elijah message for today?

____

____

What spiritual experience is necessary for the second application of Malachi's prophecy to be fulfilled?

____

____

What will happen when God's last message is given in the "spirit and power" of Elijah?

____

____

Prayer Activity

Call your prayer partner and discuss this devotional with him/her.
Pray with your prayer partner:

- **for God to continue to baptize each of you with His Holy Spirit.**
- **for God to lead His people and church to become Spirit-filled.**
- **for the individuals on your prayer list.**

INCLUDE THE FOLLOWING BIBLE VERSE IN YOUR PRAYER:
"Turn my heart toward your statutes and not toward selfish gain" (Ps. 119:36, NIV).

Cause me to love Your counsels,
and turn me from the love of money and position.

Day 21

The Church's Laodicean Problem

God gave a prophetic history of the Christian church in the book of Revelation. Revelation 2 and 3 describe seven eras of church history that apply to seven literal churches in Asia. They also apply to seven historical eras of the church, from the early apostolic church to today.

The seventh church is described in Revelation 3:14-21:

"And unto the angel of the church of the Laodiceans write; These things saith the Amen, the faithful and true witness, the beginning of the creation of God; I know thy works, that thou art neither cold nor hot: I would thou wert cold or hot. So then because thou art lukewarm, and neither cold nor hot, I will spue thee out of my mouth. Because thou sayest, I am rich, and increased with goods, and have need of nothing; and knowest not that thou art wretched, and miserable, and poor, and blind, and naked: I counsel thee to buy of me gold tried in the fire, that thou mayest be rich; and white raiment, that thou mayest be clothed, and that the shame of thy nakedness do not appear; and anoint thine eyes with eyesalve, that thou mayest see. As many as I love, I rebuke and chasten: be zealous therefore, and repent. Behold, I stand at the door, and knock: if any man hear my voice, and open the door, I will come in to him, and will sup with him, and he with me. To him that overcometh will I grant to sit with me in my throne, even as I also overcame, and am set down with my Father in his throne."

Today's church era is called Laodicea. The city of Laodicea was known for its therapeutic hot and cold hydrotherapy baths. The benefits of hydrotherapy are well understood today, and this is significant when we consider that God describes today's church as lukewarm, and neither hot nor cold (verse 16). This displeases God very much, so much so that if the church remains in this lukewarm condition, God will spew her out of His mouth.

Why is this lukewarm condition so serious in God's sight? The answer is seen in His desire for the church. God desires that the church be either hot or cold—He desires the church to be of "therapeutic" value on this earth. You see, a lukewarm church is not therapeutic—it offers little benefit to those who come in contact with it. God wants the church to bring life everywhere it goes.

This is similar to Jesus' statement that the church is to be the "salt of the earth":

"Ye are the salt of the earth: but if the salt have lost his savour, wherewith shall it be salted? it is thenceforth good for nothing, but to be cast out, and to be trodden under foot of men" (Matt. 5:13).

Both salt and hot-and-cold hydrotherapy are therapeutic. Jesus said in Revelation that those remaining in a lukewarm, nontherapeutic condition will

God desires that the church be either hot or cold.

be spewed out of His mouth. In Matthew He says that salt that has "lost his savour" will be "cast out" (5:13). Jesus is saying the same thing in both Revelation and Matthew. If the church is not therapeutic, it is of no value to God and will ultimately be cast from Him.

Jesus revealed how life was to flow from His church when He said, "He that believeth on me, as the scripture hath said, out of his belly shall flow rivers of living water." John interpreted what Jesus meant this way: "But this spake he of the Spirit, which they that believe on him should receive: for the Holy Ghost was not yet given; because that Jesus was not yet glorified" (John 7:38, 39). Through the baptism of the Holy Spirit life would flow from the church.

We can clearly see that God's warning to last-day Laodicean Christians is very serious. We must wake up to our condition and allow God to change us from nontherapeutic to therapeutic if we are to be ready to meet Jesus when He comes. The sad truth is that Laodicean Christians are not even aware of their dangerous spiritual condition:

"Because thou sayest, I am rich, and increased with goods, and have need of nothing; and knowest not that thou art wretched, and miserable, and poor, and blind, and naked" (Rev. 3:17).

Personal Reflection and Discussion

What does the Bible mean when God says the church today is lukewarm?

____

____

Why does God want the church to be either hot or cold?

____

____

What will happen to an individual who does not change from his/her lukewarm condition?

____

____

What do you think are evidences that a local congregation may be lukewarm?

____

____

What do you think may be evidence that you are a lukewarm Christian?

____

____

Prayer Activity

Call your prayer partner and discuss this devotional with him/her.
Pray with your prayer partner:

- **for God to continue to baptize each of you with His Holy Spirit.**
- **for God to bring His church out of her lukewarm, Laodicean condition.**
- **for the individuals on your prayer list.**

INCLUDE THE FOLLOWING BIBLE VERSE IN YOUR PRAYER:
"Turn thee unto me, and have mercy upon me; for I am desolate and afflicted. The troubles of my heart are enlarged: O bring thou me out of my distresses. Look upon mine affliction and my pain; and forgive all my sins" (Ps. 25:16-18).

Have mercy upon us for we are spiritually desolate and afflicted.
Forgive us our sins and bring us out of our Laodicean condition.

The Solution to the Church's Laodicean Condition

A very important question for the church today is How can we be changed from "nontherapeutic" to "therapeutic"? God's message to the Laodiceans gives us the answer. Jesus says He is standing at the door and wants into our lives:

"Behold, I stand at the door, and knock: if any man hear my voice, and open the door, I will come in to him, and will sup with him, and he with me" (Rev. 3:20).

How do we let Him in? Through the baptism of the Holy Spirit:

"And I will pray the Father, and he shall give you another Comforter, that he may abide with you for ever; even the Spirit of truth; whom the world cannot receive, because it seeth him not, neither knoweth him: but ye know him; for he dwelleth with you, and shall be in you. I will not leave you comfortless: I will come to you" (John 14:16-18).

In these verses Jesus tells the disciples that He would come to them when the Holy Spirit was available to live in them. This took place on the day of Pentecost. It is through the baptism of the Holy Spirit that Jesus lives in the believer:

A revival need be expected only in answer to prayer.

"And he that keepeth his commandments dwelleth in him, and he in him. And hereby we know that he abideth in us, by the Spirit which he hath given us" (1 John 3:24).

What will the baptism of the Holy Spirit do for a lukewarm Christian? The infilling of God's Spirit will bring revival to the recipient, and revival is the only answer to Laodicea's problem. Only by revival will the church become therapeutic to this world. Only by revival will the church come to a spiritual condition such that God can use her in a mighty way as a means of delivering men and women from the powers of darkness.

Ellen White knew the importance and urgency of revival when she wrote:

"A revival of true godliness among us is the greatest and most urgent of all our needs. To seek this should be our first work" (*Selected Messages,* bk. 1, p. 121).

She also understood the relationship between receiving the baptism of the Holy Spirit and revival:

"The baptism of the Holy Ghost as on the day of Pentecost will lead to a revival of true religion and to the performance of many wonderful works" (*Selected Messages,* bk. 2, p. 57).

The baptism of the Holy Spirit gives the Laodicean Christian the power needed to be revived spiritually, and also the power for witnessing. Jesus certainly knew the importance of what would happen when the Holy Spirit would be poured out in early-rain power on the day of Pentecost. Speaking of this, He said:

"I have come to bring fire on the earth, and how I wish it were already kindled" (Luke 12:49, NIV).

What fire was Jesus speaking of? The fire of the Holy Spirit:

"John answered, saying unto them all, I indeed baptize you with water; but one mightier than I cometh, the latchet of whose shoes I am not worthy to unloose:

he shall baptize you with the Holy Ghost and with fire" (Luke 3:16).

How does the Laodicean Christian receive the baptism of the Holy Spirit and experience revival? The same way believers always have—by prayerfully claiming God's promise. The baptism of the Holy Spirit was received by the early church on the day of Pentecost as a result of their unitedly praying for 10 days, claiming Christ's promise:

"And, being assembled together with them, commanded them that they should not depart from Jerusalem, but wait for the promise of the Father, which, saith he, ye have heard of me. For John truly baptized with water; but ye shall be baptized with the Holy Ghost not many days hence." "But ye shall receive power, after that the Holy Ghost is come upon you: and ye shall be witnesses unto me both in Jerusalem, and in all Judaea, and in Samaria, and unto the uttermost part of the earth." "These all continued with one accord in prayer and supplication, with the women, and Mary the mother of Jesus, and with his brethren" (Acts 1:4, 5, 8, 14).

Ellen White confirmed this:

"A revival need be expected only in answer to prayer" (*Selected Messages,* bk. 1, p. 121).

Every Christian today needs to pray the prayer of David: "Wilt thou not revive us again: that thy people may rejoice in thee?" (Ps. 85:6).

Personal Reflection and Discussion

What is the only solution to the Laodicean problem?

____

____

What does Ellen White say is the greatest need of the church?

____

____

What two things must the church do in order to experience genuine revival?

____

____

How did the disciples receive the reviving power of the Holy Spirit?

____

____

What do you think will be seen in the life of a Spirit-filled, revived church and Christian?

____

____

Prayer Activity

Call your prayer partner and discuss this devotional with him/her.

Pray with your prayer partner:

- **for God to continue to baptize each of you with His Holy Spirit.**
- **for God to bring revival into your life and His church.**
- **for the individuals on your prayer list.**

INCLUDE THE FOLLOWING BIBLE VERSE IN YOUR PRAYER:
"Wilt thou not revive us again: that thy people may rejoice in thee?" (Ps. 85:6).

Revive us and make us a people who rejoice in You.

Day 23

Prayer and Evangelism

God's Word teaches that prayer is necessary for an individual and a church to experience revival:

"Wilt thou not revive us again: that thy people may rejoice in thee?" (Ps. 85:6).

Prayer is necessary for the "strong holds" of Satan to be cast down, and for the saving of the lost:

"(For the weapons of our warfare are not carnal, but mighty through God to the pulling down of strong holds;) Casting down imaginations, and every high thing that exalteth itself against the knowledge of God, and bringing into captivity every thought to the obedience of Christ" (2 Cor. 10:4, 5).

Prayer is necessary for a Christian to remain strong in the Lord:

"Praying always with all prayer and supplication in the Spirit, and watching thereunto with all perseverance and supplication for all saints" (Eph. 6:18).

I find it amazing that prayer, which seems so powerless and insignificant to the natural person, is so necessary and powerful for the spiritual person. Why is prayer so important and necessary in God's work?

Those who we know are outside of Christ and living under Satan's power are in a very dangerous position. Their eternal destiny is in jeopardy if they don't change. Yet of themselves they are powerless to change. Paul describes them as those whose minds have been blinded by Satan:

"But if our gospel be hid, it is hid to them that are lost: in whom the god of this world hath blinded the minds of them which believe not, lest the light of the glorious gospel of Christ, who is the image of God, should shine unto them" (2 Cor. 4:3, 4).

The lost are blinded to the gospel because it is "hid" from their view. The word translated *hid* is the Greek word *kalupsis,* which refers to a "veil."

The key to saving the lost is to remove this veil that blinds them. By adding the prefix *apo* to the Greek word for *veil* the word becomes "revelation," or "unveiling." Hence, the lost need an unveiling, or a revelation of God's truth. The lost don't need more information—they need an unveiling of their understanding so they can "see" the truth of the gospel. An important question, then, is How can this unveiling happen in the lives of the lost?

Intercessory prayer will remove from the mind of the unbeliever the veil causing spiritual blindness. Satan has false imaginations, or thoughts and strongholds, well established in the minds of the lost. The good news is that God has given the Christian the authority to pull down Satan's strongholds and to bring "into captivity every thought to the obedience of Christ" (2 Cor. 10:4, 5). These two verses are very important when it comes to understanding the place of intercessory prayer for the lost. Ellen White clearly understood the necessity of prayer for those outside of Christ when she wrote:

"Through much prayer you must labor for souls, for this is the only method by which you can reach hearts. It is not your work, but the work of Christ who is by your side, that impresses hearts" (*Evangelism,* p. 341).

The Praying Church Sourcebook gives the following list of what God's will is for the unsaved. As believers in Christ we have the right to press these requests before the throne of grace on behalf of the lost. Include in your prayer the following:

- That God will draw them to Himself:

"No man can come to me, except the Father which hath sent me draw him: and I will raise him up at the last day" (John 6:44).

- That they seek to know God:

"That they should seek the Lord, if haply they might feel after him, and find him, though he be not far from every one of us" (Acts 17:27).

- That they believe the Word of God:

"For this cause also thank we God without ceasing, because, when ye received the word of God which ye heard of us, ye received it not as the word of men, but as it is in truth, the word of God, which effectually worketh also in you that believe" (1 Thess. 2:13).

- That Satan is bound from blinding them to the truth and his influences in their life be cast down (2 Cor. 4:4; 10:4, 5, quoted above).

- That the Holy Spirit works in them:

"And when he is come, he will reprove the world of sin, and of righteousness, and of judgment: of sin, because they believe not on me; of righteousness, because I go to my Father, and ye see me no more; of judgment, because the prince of this world is judged. I have yet many things to say unto you, but ye cannot bear them now. Howbeit when he, the Spirit of truth, is come, he will guide you into all truth: for he shall not speak of himself; but whatsoever he shall hear, that shall he speak: and he will show you things to come" (John 16:8-13).

- That they turn from sin:

"Repent ye therefore, and be converted, that your sins may be blotted out, when the times of refreshing shall come from the presence of the Lord" (Acts 3:19).

- That they believe in Christ as Savior:

"But as many as received him, to them gave he power to become the sons of God, even to them that believe on his name" (John 1:12).

- That they obey Christ as Lord:

"Not every one that saith unto me, Lord, Lord, shall enter into the kingdom of heaven; but he that doeth the will of my Father which is in heaven" (Matt. 7:21).

- That they take root and grow in Christ:

"As ye have therefore received Christ Jesus the Lord, so walk ye in him: Rooted and built up in him, and stablished in the faith, as ye have been taught, abounding therein with thanksgiving" (Col. 2:6, 7).

Personal Reflection and Discussion

How necessary is prayer in God's work of saving the lost?

What does Ellen White say about prayer for the lost?

What does prayer do for those we are witnessing to?

How do you plan to apply the principles of prayer for those on your prayer list?

Prayer Activity

Call your prayer partner and discuss this devotional with him/her.
Pray with your prayer partner:

- **for God to continue to baptize each of you with His Holy Spirit.**
- **for God to bring revival into your life and His church.**
- **for God to lead you to become a true prayer warrior for the lost.**
- **for the individuals on your prayer list.**

INCLUDE THE FOLLOWING BIBLE VERSE IN YOUR PRAYER:
"And let the beauty of the Lord our God be upon us: and establish thou the work of our hands upon us; yea, the work of our hands establish thou it" (Ps. 90:17).

May Your character be seen in our lives.
Bless our efforts to advance Your kingdom
in this congregation and our community.

Day 24

Christ's Method of Evangelism

Ellen White gave us a very clear description of Christ's witnessing method:

"The Saviour mingled with men as one who desired their good. He showed His sympathy for them, ministered to their needs, and won their confidence. Then He bade them, 'Follow Me'" (*Ministry of Healing,* p. 143).

Since this was Christ's method of witnessing, when we receive the baptism of the Holy Spirit and Christ begins living more fully in us, He will begin seeking to manifest this method of witnessing through us. He will begin leading us to "mingle" with those in our circle of family and friends, putting in our heart a desire "for their good." The greatest good is for them to come to know Jesus Christ as their Savior.

Christ's method was to take the initiative in contacting those around Him. He wants you and me to do the same. If you find this difficult you need to continue to pray for the Lord to help you with this, and He will! Remember, it is Jesus in you who prompts you to do this. As you continue to yield yourself to His control in every area of your life, your witnessing will become more and more like His method.

When we continue to pray for the baptism of the Holy Spirit, more and more of the love of God will be manifested in our hearts:

"And hope maketh not ashamed; because the love of God is shed abroad in our hearts by the Holy Ghost which is given unto us" (Rom. 5:5).

This love will be seen in our ministry to others. They will begin to gain confidence that we really do care for them and will be willing to share with us the things that concern them. Everyone has hurts, disappointed dreams, frustrations, and problems with which they are struggling. This is the very reason Christ has led you to them. He knows their needs, and knows that you have the answer for them. Christ wants to reveal that answer through you to them. He wants to reveal Himself to them through you. Ellen White wrote concerning this:

"Christian sociability is altogether too little cultivated by God's people. . . . Especially should those who have tasted the love of Christ develop their social powers, for in this way they may win souls to the Saviour" (*Testimonies for the Church,* vol. 6, p. 172).

"So it is through personal contact and association that men are reached by the saving power of the gospel" (*Thoughts From the Mount of Blessing,* p. 36).

How does this all apply to the Spirit-filled Christian? First, pray for Christ to continue to fill you with His Spirit and give you the passion for souls that He has. Make a list of those in your circle of family and friends who you feel do not know Christ, or who may be a Christian but do not know the important message of Christ's second coming. Begin praying for these individuals every day, applying the prayer principles listed in the previous devotional. Next, pray that God will provide the opportunity for you to begin coming close to them to help them in some way. We must be willing to invest the time and energy it takes to come close to people. Our interest in them must be genuine, truly caring for them and wanting to help them. When in contact with those you are praying for, look for the openings God gives you to share with them.

Always remember that God is already seeking to

draw their minds and interests to Himself. In many cases He just needs us to make ourselves available for Him to speak a word of encouragement to them. God will give you the words to speak. He knows what they need to hear, and Holy Spirit power will attend the words you speak.

Personal Reflection and Discussion

List the elements of Christ's witnessing method.

____

____

Why do you think Christ chose this method for witnessing?

____

____

What should Christians do if they don't have the desire to witness for Christ?

____

____

What specifically should the Christian ask God to do in relation to witnessing?

____

____

How do you plan to apply Christ's witnessing method?

____

Prayer Activity

Call your prayer partner and discuss this devotional with him/her.
Pray with your prayer partner:

- **for God to continue to baptize each of you with His Holy Spirit.**
- **for God to bring revival into your life and His church.**
- **for God to lead you to witness as Christ witnessed to others.**
- **for the individuals on your prayer list.**

INCLUDE THE FOLLOWING BIBLE VERSE IN YOUR PRAYER:
"So is my word that goes out from my mouth: It will not return to me empty, but will accomplish what I desire and achieve the purpose for which I sent it" (Isa. 55:11, NIV).

Bless Your Word that has been preached and taught to this congregation.
May it accomplish the purpose for which You sent it.

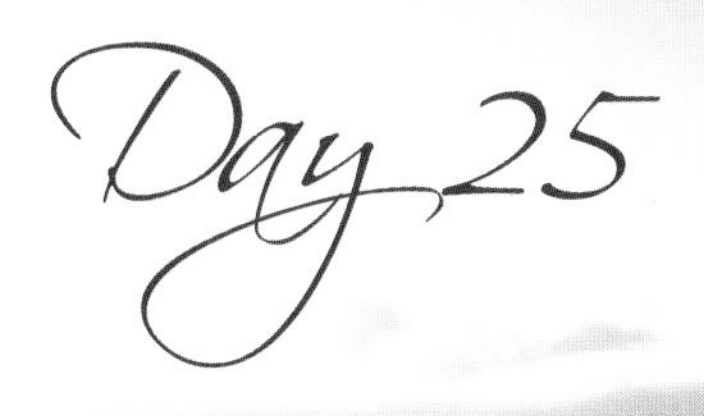

The Path to Discovery

The abiding-in-Christ teaching in the Bible is one of the most important truths that a Christian can understand. Everything hinges on experiencing the reality of abiding in Christ and Christ abiding in the believer. However, every Christian who discovers this glorious truth of Christ in us has followed a similar path as their fellow travelers. They had accepted Christ as their Savior but were burdened and bewildered by their Christian walk that was so sporadic in obedience and unfruitful in service. They longed for a consistently faithful walk with their Lord, but never found it. They struggled with besetting sins, but the sins seemed to win the battle. They prayed and studied their Bibles, but that didn't seem to bring the victory they longed for. After perhaps years of struggle, they came to the point of despair and weariness. Their sense of failure was overwhelming. The life of continual victory over sin seemed impossible to attain. Then one day they discovered the reality of the mystery of union with Christ—Christ living in them. Once discovered, they were amazed at how simple this marvelous truth is, yet it had eluded their understanding for years. After this discovery their life was never again the same. Their joy in the Lord was deep and abiding. Their life was now consistently victorious, even over besetting sins. They no longer felt burdened or anxious in their service for the Lord, and their service became the most fruitful.

The truth of abiding in Christ and His abiding in us, and how we are to experience a victorious Christian life is so simple—and yet so elusive—that most Christians have never discovered it to the fullest. Today God is calling us to this amazing experience in Christ. Why? Jesus is coming soon! All who are ready to meet Him will be just like Him:

"Beloved, now are we the sons of God, and it doth not yet appear what we shall be: but we know that, when he shall appear, we shall be like him; for we shall see him as he is" (1 John 3:2).

Their daily experience will have had to become one of complete victory in Christ if they are to be "like" Jesus when He comes:

"For even hereunto were ye called: because Christ also suffered for us, leaving us an example, that ye should follow his steps: who did no sin, neither was guile found in his mouth: who, when he was reviled, reviled not again; when he suffered, he threatened not; but committed himself to him that judgeth righteously" (1 Peter 2:21-23).

Therefore, this wonderful biblical truth is of no small consequence to Christians living in our day. Jesus is coming soon, and God is calling us to a much higher experience with Him than most of us have ever had. This devotional section is dedicated to the goal of leading all who read it to understand and experience the abiding God is offering to us; Christ in us, the hope of glory for His people:

"To whom God would make known what is the riches of the glory of this mystery among the Gentiles; which is Christ in you, the hope of glory" (Col. 1:27).

When this truth is understood and discovered, the believer will proclaim from the depths of his heart, "Christ did it all." The deliverance Christ gives lays all human boasting in the dust. Man can claim no glory for the victories over temptation and sin. All the glory will go to God and will be proclaimed throughout all eternity:

"That no flesh should glory in his presence. But of him are ye in Christ Jesus, who of God is made unto us wisdom, and righteousness, and sanctification, and redemption: that, according as it is written, He that glorieth, let him glory in the Lord" (1 Cor. 1:29-31).

Personal Reflection and Discussion

Describe the path most Christians who have discovered the truth of "Christ in you, the hope of glory", have followed.

____

____

How will understanding and experiencing this truth change the Christian's life?

____

____

Why is this truth essential for the Christian to understand and experience?

____

____

How desirous are you to understand and experience the truth of abiding in Christ and Christ abiding in you?

____

____

Prayer Activity

Call your prayer partner and discuss this devotional with him/her.
Pray with your prayer partner:

- **for God to continue to baptize each of you with His Holy Spirit.**
- **for God to bring revival into your life and His church.**
- **for God to open your understanding of the biblical truth of abiding in Christ.**
- **for the individuals on your prayer list.**

INCLUDE THE FOLLOWING BIBLE VERSE IN YOUR PRAYER:
"See, darkness covers the earth and thick darkness is over the peoples, but the Lord rises upon you and his glory appears over you. Nations will come to your light, and kings to the brightness of your dawn" (Isa. 60:2, 3, NIV).

Bring us out of our spiritual darkness.
Lord, arise in our midst and reveal the glory of Your character through us.
Draw many in our community to the light of truth You have given us.

Day 26

The Christian's Struggle

I titled today's devotional, "The Christian's Struggle," because the nonbeliever doesn't have the struggle that the Christian has. The unconverted man doesn't have the Spirit of God and is controlled only by his carnal mind. According to Paul, the carnal mind is "enmity against God: for it is not subject to the law of God, neither indeed can be" (Rom. 8:7). The nonchristian does not obey rules or laws because God has put it in his heart to do so. He obeys for personal, selfish reasons, because of social pressure, etc. Or perhaps he was raised in a principled home and has a conscience that leads him to live a respectable life.

The Christian, on the other hand, obeys God because the Spirit of God has put the desire to obey in his heart:

"But God be thanked, that ye were the servants of sin, but ye have obeyed from the heart that form of doctrine which was delivered you" (Rom. 6:17).

The born-again individual very much wants to carry out God's will in his life. Paul calls this delighting "in the law of God after the inward man" (Rom. 7:22). Under the new covenant promise, the Holy Spirit begins writing God's law in his heart and mind:

"For finding fault with them, he saith, Behold, the days come, saith the Lord, when I will make a new covenant with the house of Israel and with the house of Judah: Not according to the covenant that I made with their fathers in the day when I took them by the hand to lead them out of the land of Egypt; because they continued not in my covenant, and I regarded them not, saith the Lord. For this is the covenant that I will make with the house of Israel after those days, saith the Lord; I will put my laws into their mind, and write them in their hearts: and I will be to them a God, and they shall be to me a people" (Heb. 8:8-10).

"Forasmuch as ye are manifestly declared to be the epistle of Christ ministered by us, written not with ink, but with the Spirit of the living God; not in tables of stone, but in fleshly tables of the heart" (2 Cor. 3:3).

However, the new believer discovers very quickly that there is another very strong desire in him—the desire for sin. Now that he has the Spirit of God, he is aware of his sinful desires, whereas before, many of those desires didn't really concern him. So the Christian discovers that there are now two natures residing in him: one that desires to follow sin, and the other that desires to obey God. Paul very clearly describes this intense conflict, experienced by every Christian, in Romans 7:14-25:

"For we know that the law is spiritual: but I am carnal, sold under sin. For that which I do I allow not: for what I would, that do I not; but what I hate, that do I. If then I do that which I would not, I consent unto the law that it is good. Now then it is no more I that do it, but sin that dwelleth in me. For I know that in me (that is, in my flesh,) dwelleth no good thing: for to will is present with me; but how to perform that which is good I find not. For the good that I would I do not: but the evil which I would not, that I do. Now if I do that I would not, it is no more I that do it, but sin that dwelleth in me. I find then a law, that, when I would do good, evil is present with me. For I delight in the law of God after the inward man: but I see another law in my members, warring against the law of my mind, and bringing me into captivity to the law of sin which is in my members. O wretched man that I am! who shall deliver me from the body of this death? I thank God through Jesus Christ our Lord. So then with the mind I myself serve the law of God; but with the flesh the law of sin."

Every Christian can identify with the struggle Paul describes. Christians often experience this struggle day after day, month after month, and year after year, and never obtain the victory they want to have over sin. Every Christian is well aware of the fact that there is a "law of sin" dwelling within them that is waging war against the God-given desire to obey His law. As Paul states, he delighted in God's law. He very much wanted to obey God in all things; however, he found that it was impossible for him to do so. His sinful nature constantly sought to make him a slave to the law of sin.

Recognizing the impossibility of obeying God because of the power of sin in his life, Paul cries out, "What a wretched man I am! Who will rescue me from this body of death?" He then declares that deliverance from the law of sin can happen "through Jesus Christ our Lord" (verses 24, 25, NIV).

In Romans 8:1-4, Paul gives the solution to this problem in the believer's life:

"There is therefore now no condemnation to them which are in Christ Jesus, who walk not after the flesh, but after the Spirit. For the law of the Spirit of life in Christ Jesus hath made me free from the law of sin and death. For what the law could not do, in that it was weak through the flesh, God sending his own Son in the likeness of sinful flesh, and for sin, condemned sin in the flesh: that the righteousness of the law might be fulfilled in us, who walk not after the flesh, but after the Spirit."

The solution to the Christian's dilemma is to allow Christ Jesus, through the law of the Spirit of life, to set us free from the law of sin and death. Put another way, we must let Jesus live out His life in us through the baptism of the Holy Spirit. This is what Paul calls "walking in the Spirit." He further elaborates on this in his letter to the Galatians:

"This I say then, Walk in the Spirit, and ye shall not fulfil the lust of the flesh. For the flesh lusteth against the Spirit, and the Spirit against the flesh: and these are contrary the one to the other: so that ye cannot do the things that ye would" (Gal. 5:16, 17).

Paul tells us that the righteous requirements of the law will be fulfilled "in us" when we have Jesus living in us through the baptism of the Holy Spirit:

"That the righteousness of the law might be fulfilled in us, who walk not after the flesh, but after the Spirit" (Rom. 8:4).

Personal Reflection and Discussion

What is the difference between the Christian's and nonchristian's heartfelt attitude toward sin?

How does Paul describe the Christian's struggle with sin?

What does Paul say is the solution to the Christian's struggle with sin?

What has been your experience with your personal struggle with sin?

Prayer Activity

Call your prayer partner and discuss this devotional with him/her.

Pray with your prayer partner:

- **for God to continue to baptize each of you with His Holy Spirit.**
- **for God to bring revival into your life and His church.**
- **for God to lead you to experience genuine abiding in Christ for victory over sin.**
- **for the individuals on your prayer list.**

INCLUDE THE FOLLOWING BIBLE VERSE IN YOUR PRAYER:

"That the God of our Lord Jesus Christ, the Father of glory, may give unto you the spirit of wisdom and revelation in the knowledge of him: the eyes of your understanding being enlightened; that ye may know what is the hope of his calling, and what the riches of the glory of his inheritance in the saints, and what is the exceeding greatness of his power to usward who believe, according to the working of his mighty power" (Eph. 1:17-19).

Give us the wisdom and understanding we need to fully love and appreciate You.
Open our eyes to see our sinfulness and the greatness of Your mercy and forgiveness.
Lead us to understand the wonderful hope we have in Jesus.
Open our eyes to see and believe in Your great power that is available to us
to overcome anything Satan brings into our lives.
By Your power, bring us back to You and revive us.

Day 27

Sin's Power Broken

There are many aspects to the good news of the gospel of Jesus Christ. One is that at the cross the power of the sinful nature was broken for all who accept Christ and believe:

"Knowing this, that our old man is crucified with him, that the body of sin might be destroyed, that henceforth we should not serve sin" (Rom. 6:6). "Likewise reckon ye also yourselves to be dead indeed unto sin, but alive unto God through Jesus Christ our Lord" (verse 11).

When Jesus died on the cross, the power of the sinful nature in every believer's life was broken. This is an historical fact. However, it becomes a reality in the Christian's life only if he believes it.

This means that the unloving you, the unforgiving you, the angry you, the lustful you, the anxious you—the list could go on and on—died at the cross. That is wonderful news! It means that you do not have to be controlled by your unloving attitudes, your unforgiveness, anger, lustful thoughts and desires, etc. The power of these sinful desires, attitudes, and behaviors is broken.

The problem most Christians encounter when they read these Bible verses is that they conclude they should then be able to obey God with His help. For example, consider the Christian who has a struggle with anger. He reasons that if the power of his sinful anger was broken at the cross he now can stop being angry when something happens to cause him to become angry. He feels great relief, confident that now he will finally have the victory. Soon something happens to cause him to feel anger. Perhaps someone cuts him off while driving, or someone says something very unkind to him. Immediately anger arises. He puts forth efforts to subdue it, but he finds that it keeps lingering. He doesn't want these feelings, but seems helpless to get rid of them. He begins questioning himself about why anger is still arising in his feelings. He concludes that he must not have asked God or received from God enough of His power to assist him in his efforts to overcome the anger. So he pleads with God to remove the anger, to give him the power needed, to give him the victory. Even so, he continues to experience the same pattern of being overcome by his besetting sins. More confusion and feelings of defeat set in. Again he questions his sincerity and has no peace in his walk with the Lord.

It is very true that the power of our sinful nature was broken at the cross. However, this does not mean that if we now believe this we can begin obeying God by putting forth efforts to do so. Remember, we have no ability in and of ourselves to obey God, even though the overwhelming influence of our sinful nature was broken at the cross. Simply knowing and believing that truth is not enough. No. There is only one way we will have the victory we long for. The victory over temptation and sin will take place in our lives only as we believe the truth of the crucifixion of our sinful nature and also allow Christ to give us His victory. We must understand that we will be victorious over sin and temptation only as we allow Him to live out His life of victory in us:

"For they being ignorant of God's righteousness, and going about to establish their own righteousness, have not submitted themselves unto the righteousness of God. For Christ is the end of the law for righteousness to every one that believeth" (Rom. 10:3, 4).

"For to me to live is Christ, and to die is gain" (Phil. 1:21).

Personal Reflection and Discussion

What happened to the power of the Christian's sinful nature at the cross?

If one knows and believes this truth, does it mean he/she can now begin obeying God consistently? Why, or why not?

What must the Christian also believe in order to overcome sin consistently?

Have you ever been tempted to believe that you are not really a Christian because of the sin problem in your life?

Have you ever asked God to remove a particular sin in your life, but He didn't seem to hear or answer you, and your struggle with it continued?

Prayer Activity

Call your prayer partner and discuss this devotional with him/her.

- **Pray with your prayer partner:**
- **for God to continue to baptize each of you with His Holy Spirit.**
- **for God to bring revival into your life and His church.**
- **for God to give you a revelation of how you are to let Jesus live out His life of victory in and through you.**
- **for the individuals on your prayer list.**

INCLUDE THE FOLLOWING BIBLE VERSE IN YOUR PRAYER:
"That he [God] would grant you, according to the riches of his glory, to be strengthened with might by his Spirit in the inner man; That Christ may dwell in your hearts by faith; that ye being rooted and grounded in love, may be able to comprehend with all saints what is the breadth, and length, and depth, and height; and to know the love of Christ, which passeth knowledge, that ye might be filled with all the fulness of God" (Eph. 3:16-19).

Fill us with Your Spirit. Strengthen us by the power of Your Spirit so that we can stand against all the attacks of the enemy.
Fill us with Your love and open our eyes to understand the love of Christ so we will reveal Christ's love to others by our words and actions.

Day 28

Christ Gives the Victory

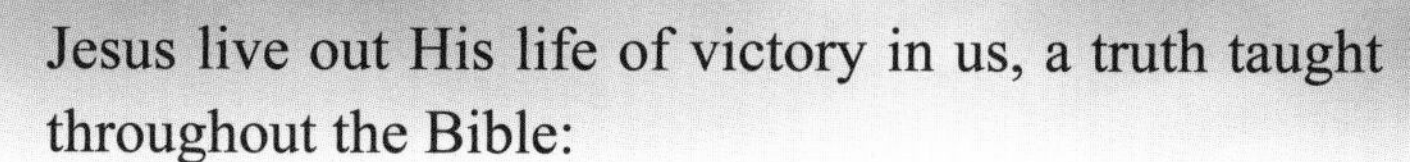

Until the Christian comes to understand and experience what it means to let Christ give him His victory, he will not experience the consistently obedient life he desires. In today's devotional I will present how to let Christ live out His victorious life in you. When you come to understand and experience this truth, your Christian life will never again be the same. Instead of a life of sporadic obedience and broken promises to God, you will, in time, experience a life of victory through Christ over every temptation and sin that Satan brings your way.

Is such a consistently obedient life really possible? Can we truly have victory over every temptation and sin in our life? That is the kind of life God calls us to live:

"Knowing this, that our old man is crucified with him, that the body of sin might be destroyed, that henceforth we should not serve sin" (Rom. 6:6). "Likewise reckon ye also yourselves to be dead indeed unto sin, but alive unto God through Jesus Christ our Lord. Let not sin therefore reign in your mortal body, that ye should obey it in the lusts thereof. Neither yield ye your members as instruments of unrighteousness unto sin: but yield yourselves unto God, as those that are alive from the dead, and your members as instruments of righteousness unto God. For sin shall not have dominion over you: for ye are not under the law, but under grace" (verses 11-14).

Ellen White agrees:

"He who has not sufficient faith in Christ to believe that He can keep him from sinning, has not the faith that will give him an entrance into the kingdom of God" (*Manuscript 161,* 1897, p. 9).

So what is the answer to how we can live a consistently victorious Christian life? The answer is to let Jesus live out His life of victory in us, a truth taught throughout the Bible:

"I have set the Lord always before me: because he is at my right hand, I shall not be moved" (Ps. 16:8).

"Thou wilt keep him in perfect peace, whose mind is stayed on thee: because he trusteth in thee. Trust ye in the Lord for ever: for in the Lord Jehovah is everlasting strength" (Isa. 26:3, 4).

"Abide in me, and I in you. As the branch cannot bear fruit of itself, except it abide in the vine; no more can ye, except ye abide in me. I am the vine, ye are the branches: He that abideth in me, and I in him, the same bringeth forth much fruit: for without me ye can do nothing" (John 15:4, 5).

Christ's mind was filled with pure, holy, virtuous thoughts. If we have asked Christ to live in us through the baptism of the Holy Spirit, if we believe He does, and if we believe He will manifest His love—His pure, holy, virtuous thoughts in our minds—He will do just that. It is a matter of faith; believing He will truly manifest Himself in our lives. Paul recognized this fact when he wrote:

"I am crucified with Christ: nevertheless I live; yet not I, but Christ liveth in me: and the life which I now live in the flesh I live by the faith of the Son of God, who loved me, and gave himself for me" (Gal. 2:20).

"That he would grant you, according to the riches of his glory, to be strengthened with might by his Spirit in the inner man; that Christ may dwell in your hearts by faith" (Eph. 3:16, 17).

In order to experience true abiding in Christ you must realize that Jesus does literally abide in you. He said that He does, and you can believe Him. This happens as you daily receive the baptism of the Holy Spirit:

"And I will pray the Father, and he shall give you another Comforter, that he may abide with you for ever; even the Spirit of truth; whom the world cannot receive, because it seeth him not, neither knoweth him: but ye know him; for he dwelleth with you, and shall be in you. I will not leave you comfortless: I will come to you" (John 14:16-18).

"And he that keepeth his commandments dwelleth in him, and he in him. And hereby we know that he abideth in us, by the Spirit which he hath given us" (1 John 3:24).

With Jesus living in you, you have His mind:

"For who hath known the mind of the Lord, that he may instruct him? but we have the mind of Christ" (1 Cor. 2:16).

We have His love, joy, peace, patience, gentleness, goodness, faith, meekness, temperance—all the fruit of the Spirit:

"But the fruit of the Spirit is love, joy, peace, longsuffering, gentleness, goodness, faith, Meekness, temperance: against such there is no law" (Gal. 5:22, 23).

Through Jesus living in us via the baptism of the Holy Spirit, we have His likes and dislikes, His pure thoughts, His forgiveness—the list could go on and on. Every virtue of Christ is in you through Christ abiding in you.

How is the Christian to apply this truth? Simply put, the steps are these. When you become aware of a temptation to sin:

1. Choose to turn your mind immediately away from the temptation:

"Finally, brethren, whatsoever things are true, whatsoever things are honest, whatsoever things are just, whatsoever things are pure, whatsoever things are lovely, whatsoever things are of good report; if there be any virtue, and if there be any praise, think on these things" (Phil. 4:8).

2. Believe that the power of your sinful nature's attraction to the temptation to control you is broken.

3. Believe Jesus is in you, and ask Him to manifest His virtue in you in relation to the temptation. Be specific.

4. Believe that He will manifest Himself in that manner, rest in that belief, and don't fight the temptation. When we fight the temptation we are actually focusing on it and trying to resist it in our own strength rather than looking to Jesus for the victory:

"Wherefore seeing we also are compassed about with so great a cloud of witnesses, let us lay aside every weight, and the sin which doth so easily beset us, and let us run with patience the race that is set before us, looking unto Jesus the author and finisher of our faith; who for the joy that was set before him endured the cross, despising the shame, and is set down at the right hand of the throne of God" (Heb. 12:1, 2).

5. Thank Him for the deliverance He has just given you.

Personal Reflection and Discussion

According to the Bible and Ellen White, is a consistently obedient life possible?

____

What does the Bible teach about Jesus living in the Christian? Give Bible verses.

____

What is the benefit to you of having Christ live in you?

____

____

What are the steps to allow Jesus to give you victory over a temptation?

____

____

How do you plan to apply this teaching in your personal life?

____

____

Prayer Activity

Call your prayer partner and discuss this devotional with him/her.
Pray with your prayer partner:

- **for God to continue to baptize each of you with His Holy Spirit.**
- **for God to bring revival into your life and His church.**
- **for God to lead you to let Jesus live out His victorious life in you when you are tempted to sin.**
- **for the individuals on your prayer list.**

INCLUDE THE FOLLOWING BIBLE VERSE IN YOUR PRAYER:
"Now unto him that is able to do exceeding abundantly above all that we ask or think, according to the power that worketh in us" (Eph. 3:20).

Open our understanding that we will never doubt Your power to deliver us from sin, to revive us individually and as a church, and to spread the gospel in our community.
Help us to believe that the greatest power in this universe lives in us through Your Holy Spirit.

Day 29

Righteousness by Faith

Righteousness by faith is simply looking to Jesus to manifest His righteous life of victory in our life. God wants us to look to Christ for victory, not to ourselves:

"Wherefore seeing we also are compassed about with so great a cloud of witnesses, let us lay aside every weight, and the sin which doth so easily beset us, and let us run with patience the race that is set before us, looking unto Jesus the author and finisher of our faith; who for the joy that was set before him endured the cross, despising the shame, and is set down at the right hand of the throne of God" (Heb. 12:1, 2).

This is true righteousness by faith and is God's will for every Christian. Oswald Chambers, a well-known Christian author, clearly presented this wonderful truth in the July 23 reading of his daily devotional, *My Utmost for His Highest:*

"But of Him you are in Christ Jesus, who became for us . . . sanctification" (1 Cor. 1:30, NKJV).

"The Life Side: The mystery of sanctification is that the perfect qualities of Jesus Christ are imparted as a gift to me, not gradually, but instantly once I enter by faith into the realization that He 'became for [me] . . . sanctification. . . .' Sanctification means nothing less than the holiness of Jesus becoming mine and being exhibited in my life.

"The most wonderful secret of living a holy life does not lie in imitating Jesus, but in letting the perfect qualities of Jesus exhibit themselves in my human flesh. Sanctification is 'Christ in you . . .' (Col. 1:27). It is *His* wonderful life that is imparted to me in sanctification—imparted by faith as a sovereign gift of God's grace. Am I willing for God to make sanctification as real in me as it is in His Word?

"Sanctification means the impartation of the holy qualities of Jesus Christ to me. It is the gift of His patience, love, holiness, faith, purity, and godliness that is exhibited in and through every sanctified soul. Sanctification is not drawing from Jesus the power to be holy—it is drawing from Jesus the very holiness that was exhibited in Him, and that He now exhibits in me. Sanctification is an impartation, not an imitation. Imitation is something altogether different. The perfection of everything is in Jesus Christ, and the mystery of sanctification is that all the perfect qualities of Jesus are at my disposal. Consequently, I slowly but surely begin to live a life of inexpressible order, soundness, and holiness—'. . . kept by the power of God . . .' (1Peter 1:5)."

Do you see the beauty of this truth? Our part is to look to Jesus in trusting faith, believing God's promise to manifest Christ and His righteousness in us. Our only part is to choose to let this happen and believe it will happen. When unrighteous desires and temptations come, we are not to fight against them. We are to turn to Christ who is living within us and to ask Him to manifest His own righteousness (Heb. 12:1, 2). Then we are to wait in faith believing He will do it.

When Christ is fully manifest in His people then the earth will be enlightened with His glory or character:

"And after these things I saw another angel come down from heaven, having great power; and the earth was lightened with his glory" (Rev. 18:1).

Then His people will be just like Jesus:

"Beloved, now are we the sons of God, and it doth not yet appear what we shall be: but we know that, when he shall appear, we shall be like him; for we shall see him as he is" (1 John 3:2).

Then when He returns they will be able to stand in the very presence of Christ in all His glory and not be consumed. This is God's promise to His children, and it will be fulfilled as we learn to look to Jesus in faith for this marvelous manifestation of Himself in us:

"Now unto him that is able to keep you from falling, and to present you faultless before the presence of his glory with exceeding joy" (Jude 24).

Personal Reflection and Discussion

According to today's devotional study, what is God's will for every Christian?

____

____

What is true righteousness by faith?

____

____

Describe in your own words what Oswald Chambers wrote.

____

____

How do you plan to apply righteousness by faith to your personal life?

____

Prayer Activity

Call your prayer partner and discuss this devotional with him/her.
Pray with your prayer partner:

- **for God to continue to baptize each of you with His Holy Spirit.**
- **for God to bring revival into your life and His church.**
- **for God to lead you to let Jesus manifest Himself fully in your life so that you truly experience righteousness by faith in Christ alone.**
- **for the individuals on your prayer list.**

INCLUDE THE FOLLOWING BIBLE VERSE IN YOUR PRAYER:
"For I will pour water on the thirsty land, and streams on the dry ground; I will pour out my Spirit on your offspring, and my blessing on your descendants. They will spring up like grass in a meadow, like poplar trees by flowing streams" (Isa. 44:3, 4).

We are as a dry ground spiritually—
pour out Your Spirit on us and cause us to revive and grow
into the fullness of Christ.

Day 30

God's Commandments and Abiding in Christ

Obedience to God's commandments and abiding in Christ go hand-in-hand. You cannot have one without the other. Jesus said: "If ye keep my commandments, ye shall abide in my love; even as I have kept my Father's commandments, and abide in his love" (John 15:10).

Jesus, the Holy Spirit, and God's law are inseparable. When we abide in Christ and He abides in us the Ten Commandments will become an integral part of our life because the Holy Spirit will be writing them on our heart:

"Forasmuch as ye are manifestly declared to be the epistle of Christ ministered by us, written not with ink, but with the Spirit of the living God; not in tables of stone, but in fleshly tables of the heart" (2 Cor. 3:3).

In fact, it was Jesus who, before His incarnation, gave Moses the Ten Commandments. The God who gave the commandments revealed Himself to Moses as the I AM:

"And God said unto Moses, I AM THAT I AM: and he said, Thus shalt thou say unto the children of Israel, I AM hath sent me unto you" (Ex. 3:14).

Jesus claimed to be the I AM of the Old Testament:

"Jesus said unto them, Verily, verily, I say unto you, Before Abraham was, I am" (John 8:58).

In Paul's letters we find many instructions concerning the attitudes and behaviors the Lord wants us to exhibit in our life. Paul gives very implicit instruction concerning behavior:

"That ye put off concerning the former conversation the old man, which is corrupt according to the deceitful lusts; and be renewed in the spirit of your mind; and that ye put on the new man, which after God is created in righteousness and true holiness. Wherefore putting away lying, speak every man truth with his neighbour: for we are members one of another. Be ye angry, and sin not: let not the sun go down upon your wrath: neither give place to the devil. Let him that stole steal no more: but rather let him labour, working with his hands the thing which is good, that he may have to give to him that needeth. Let no corrupt communication proceed out of your mouth, but that which is good to the use of edifying, that it may minister grace unto the hearers. And grieve not the holy Spirit of God, whereby ye are sealed unto the day of redemption. Let all bitterness, and wrath, and anger, and clamour, and evil speaking, be put away from you, with all malice: and be ye kind one to another, tenderhearted, forgiving one another, even as God for Christ's sake hath forgiven you" (Eph. 4:22-32).

Why is so much space given in the Bible to inform us of the behavior God wants us to follow? The reason is that we need to know the attitudes and behaviors He wants us to have so that we can be aware of situations when we are tempted to behave wrongly. If we didn't know God's will in these areas, we wouldn't choose to let Christ manifest that aspect of His character in us. For example, if a believer doesn't know it is wrong to hold onto anger and say something critical when someone wrongs him, he won't turn his thoughts away from the anger and critical spirit he begins to feel. He won't choose to let Christ manifest His "non-anger" and "non-critical spirit" in the situation because he is unaware that anger and a critical spirit are wrong. And so, he will not reflect Christ's character in that particular situation. He has not begun developing Christ's character within himself in that area of his life.

When Christ lives in us He will seek to live out His life in and through us. This means that He will seek to live out the Ten Commandments in our lives just as He did when He walked this earth:

"I delight to do thy will, O my God: yea, thy law is within my heart" (Ps. 40:8).

Also, the Ten Commandments are inseparably connected to love. Jesus made this very clear when He taught:

"And, behold, one came and said unto him, Good Master, what good thing shall I do, that I may have eternal life? And he said unto him, Why callest thou me good? there is none good but one, that is, God: but if thou wilt enter into life, keep the commandments. He saith unto him, Which? Jesus said, Thou shalt do no murder, Thou shalt not commit adultery, Thou shalt not steal, Thou shalt not bear false witness, Honour thy father and thy mother: and, Thou shalt love thy neighbour as thyself" (Matt. 19:16-19).

"Then one of them, which was a lawyer, asked him a question, tempting him, and saying, Master, which is the great commandment in the law? Jesus said unto him, Thou shalt love the Lord thy God with all thy heart, and with all thy soul, and with all thy mind. This is the first and great commandment. And the second is like unto it, Thou shalt love thy neighbour as thyself. On these two commandments hang all the law and the prophets" (Matt. 22:35-40).

The apostle Paul taught that love and God's Ten Commandments refer to the same experience in one's life:

"Owe no man any thing, but to love one another: for he that loveth another hath fulfilled the law. For this, Thou shalt not commit adultery, Thou shalt not kill, Thou shalt not steal, Thou shalt not bear false witness, Thou shalt not covet; and if there be any other commandment, it is briefly comprehended in this saying, namely, Thou shalt love thy neighbour as thyself. Love worketh no ill to his neighbour: therefore love is the fulfilling of the law" (Rom. 13:8-10).

The first four commandments reveal how we love God, and the last six tell us how we are to love each other. Hence, Christ abiding in us, the Ten Commandments, love, and intimately knowing Jesus are all closely related. You cannot have one without the others. John wrote of this close connection in his first letter:

"And hereby we do know that we know him, if we keep his commandments. He that saith, I know him, and keepeth not his commandments, is a liar, and the truth is not in him. But whoso keepeth his word, in him verily is the love of God perfected: hereby know we that we are in him. He that saith he abideth in him ought himself also so to walk, even as he walked" (1 John 2:3-6).

John clearly links intimately knowing Jesus, the Ten Commandments, love, and abiding in Him. He says that if we are abiding in Christ, we will be "walking," or living, as He lived. Why? Because Jesus will be living out His life in us, and our lives will be lives of obedience to God's Ten Commandments.

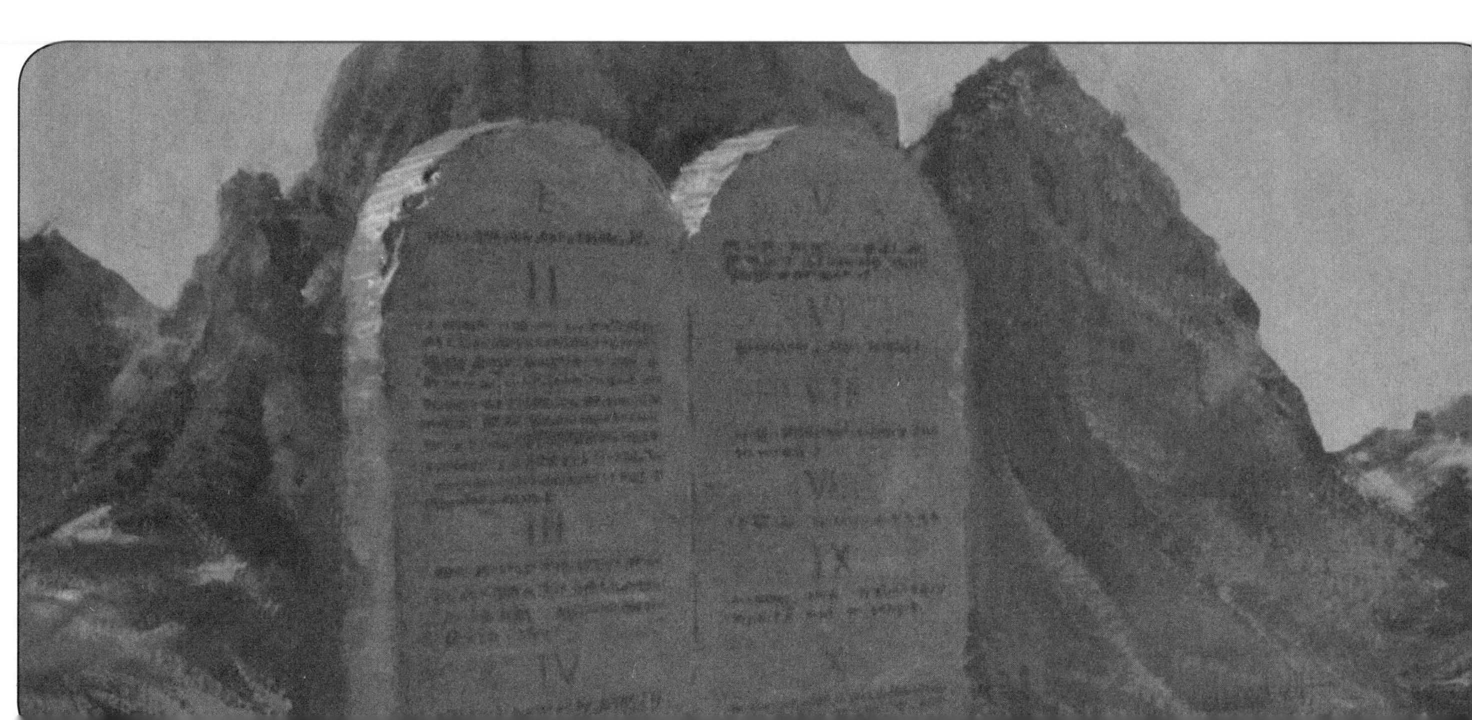

Personal Reflection and Discussion

How did Jesus connect abiding in Him with the Ten Commandments?

How did Jesus connect love with the Ten Commandments?

Who gave the Ten Commandments on Mount Sinai?

Where does God write the Ten Commandments today, and through what means?

How do you plan to apply the lesson of this devotional study to your life this week?

Prayer Activity

Call your prayer partner and discuss this devotional with him/her.
Pray with your prayer partner:

- **for God to continue to baptize each of you with His Holy Spirit.**
- **for God to bring revival into your life and His church.**
- **for God to write His Ten Commandment law in your heart, and lead you to let Jesus live out His obedience to the Ten Commandments in your life.**
- **for the individuals on your prayer list.**

INCLUDE THE FOLLOWING BIBLE VERSE IN YOUR PRAYER:
"It is time for you to act, O Lord: your law is being broken" (Ps. 119:126, NIV).

Remove our law breaking from us—give us a heart of obedience.

Day 31

Abiding in Christ and Service

Service for the Lord can become a heavy burden at times, filled with anxiety and stress, before the Christian comes to understand and experience true abiding in Christ and His abiding in him. However, once the mystery of union with Christ is experienced, everything changes. Service for the Master is a joy, and the stress and burdens are relieved.

Ellen White wrote of the great peace Jesus had when He ministered on earth. Describing His response during the storm that threatened His disciples and Him, she wrote:

"When Jesus was awakened to meet the storm, He was in perfect peace. There was no trace of fear in word or look, for no fear was in His heart. But He rested not in the possession of almighty power. It was not as the 'Master of earth and sea and sky' that He reposed in quiet. That power He had laid down, and He says, 'I can of Mine own self do nothing.' John 5:30. He trusted in the Father's might. It was in faith—faith in God's love and care—that Jesus rested, and the power of that word which stilled the storm was the power of God" (*The Desire of Ages,* p. 336).

She goes on to challenge us to trust our Lord in the same manner:

"As Jesus rested by faith in the Father's care, so we are to rest in the care of our Saviour. If the disciples had trusted in Him, they would have been kept in peace. Their fear in the time of danger revealed their unbelief. In their efforts to save themselves, they forgot Jesus; and it was only when, in despair of self-dependence, they turned to Him that He could give them help.

"How often the disciples' experience is ours! When the tempests of temptation gather, and the fierce lightnings flash, and the waves sweep over us, we battle with the storm alone, forgetting that there is One who can help us. We trust in our own strength till our hope is lost, and we are ready to perish. Then we remember Jesus, and if we call upon Him to save us, we shall not cry in vain. . . . Whether on the land or on the sea, if we have the Saviour in our hearts, there is no need of fear. Living faith in the Redeemer will smooth the sea of life, and will deliver us from danger in the way that He knows to be best" (*Ibid*).

When we are truly experiencing abiding in Christ and He abiding in us, His presence is a reality. Our resting in Him will then become real, not just a theory, and it will be consistent. All fear, worry, and stress in service or life will be gone. The burdens of ministry will be lifted, replaced with our resting in Jesus' presence. As Ellen White says We must despair of self-dependency and turn to Christ.

> ***All fear, worry, and stress in service or life will be gone.***

When we are abiding in Christ, we will have the relationship with Him that He had with His Father, which enabled Him to rest in the assurance that the Father would speak and minister through Him.

"Believest thou not that I am in the Father, and the Father in me? the words that I speak unto you I speak not of myself: but the Father that dwelleth in me, he doeth the works" (John 14:10).

Personal Reflection and Discussion

If you are fearful or overstressed in your service for the Lord, what does that indicate about you?

____

____

Was it unreasonable for the disciples to be fearful when they were in the boat in the storm? Why, or why not?

____

____

How do you usually react when trials, temptations, and difficulties come into your life?

____

____

How does God want you to react in difficult and trying situations?

____

____

How do you plan to apply the lesson of this devotional study to your life this week?

____

Prayer Activity

Call your prayer partner and discuss this devotional with him/her.

Pray with your prayer partner:

- **for God to continue to baptize each of you with His Holy Spirit.**
- **for God to bring revival into your life and His church.**
- **for God to remind you to look to Jesus and to trust Him when the next opportunity comes to serve Christ or a trial comes into your life.**
- **for the individuals on your prayer list.**

INCLUDE THE FOLLOWING BIBLE VERSE IN YOUR PRAYER:
"O taste and see that the Lord is good: blessed is the man that trusteth in him" (Ps. 34:8).

Cause us to trust in You, Lord,
and not in earthly things, and then bless us abundantly.

Day 32

The Sabbath Rest

The gospel is taught in the Creation story. In Genesis we read: "Thus the heavens and the earth were finished, and all the host of them. And on the seventh day God ended his work which he had made; and he rested on the seventh day from all his work which he had made" (Gen. 2:1, 2).

Here we discover that God worked, then rested. The situation for Adam was just the opposite. First, he entered into God's rest since the seventh-day Sabbath was his first full day of life. After entering God's rest on the seventh day, he then worked.

The same sequence is true concerning man's redemption. In Christ, God completed the work of redemption through His sinless life, death, and resurrection. Man begins experiencing God's redemptive work in his life by resting in what God has already done for him. He rests in the fact that Jesus died for his sins and has given to him eternal life as a free gift. He rests in the fact that he has Christ's righteousness covering him. He also rests in the fact that at the cross the power of his sinful nature was broken, and he is now free to serve God. Daily, he rests in the fact that Christ lives in him and will live out His life in and through him if he simply chooses to let Him.

Once the believer rests in these truths, he is able then to "work," or faithfully serve and obey God in life and ministry. This rest is necessary for him to faithfully serve God. By rest I mean that he accepts by faith what God has done for his redemption, and trusts implicitly in Christ.

In Hebrews 4 we find a similar description of the concept of rest in the story of Israel's failure to enter into God's rest during their wilderness sojourn:

"There remaineth therefore a rest to the people of God. For he that is entered into his rest, he also hath ceased from his own works, as God did from his. Let us labour therefore to enter into that rest, lest any man fall after the same example of unbelief" (Heb. 4:9-11).

God's Word is very clear about the concept of rest. When we enter into God's rest we cease our own efforts. We are told that it is important for us to seek to enter into this rest. Otherwise, we will fail in our obedience to God because of unbelief.

The only way to gain victory over temptation and sin is to rest in the fact that Jesus abides in us and to allow Him to live out His life in and through us. We must rest in that truth through belief and not hinder God's work of redemption in our life by trying to work or exert our own effort to obey. Our part is to believe and choose to let Christ live out His life in us. We are to rest in His completed work. This resting in Christ is the true meaning of the Sabbath rest God calls us to experience:

"Remember the sabbath day, to keep it holy. Six days shalt thou labour, and do all thy work: but the seventh day is the sabbath of the Lord thy God: in it thou shalt not do any work, thou, nor thy son, nor thy daughter, thy manservant, nor thy maidservant, nor thy cattle, nor thy stranger that is within thy gates: for in six days the Lord made heaven and earth, the sea, and all that in them is, and rested the seventh day: wherefore the Lord blessed the sabbath day, and hallowed it" (Ex. 20:8-11).

Our part is to choose and to believe. This requires 100 percent surrender to Christ 100 percent of the time.

Personal Reflection and Discussion

How is the gospel taught in the creation account?

____

____

What truths about Jesus are Christians to rest in?

____

____

How is resting in Jesus connected with an obedient Christian life?

____

What is the true meaning of Sabbath rest?

____

How do you plan to apply the lesson of this devotional study to your life this week?

____

____

Prayer Activity

Call your prayer partner and discuss this devotional with him/her.
Pray with your prayer partner:

- **for God to continue to baptize each of you with His Holy Spirit.**
- **for God to bring revival into your life and His church.**
- **for God to lead you to enter into the true meaning of Sabbath rest.**
- **for the individuals on your prayer list.**

INCLUDE THE FOLLOWING BIBLE VERSE IN YOUR PRAYER:
"Seek the Lord while he may be found; call on him while he is near. Let the wicked forsake his way and the evil man his thoughts. Let him turn to the Lord, and he will have mercy on him, and to our God, for he will freely pardon" (Isa. 55:6, 7, NIV).

Cause us to seek You and forsake our wicked ways and evil thoughts.
Cause us to turn to You with our whole heart.
Have mercy on us and pardon us.

Day 33

SECTION FIVE

Spirit Baptism and Fellowship

Something Missing

The baptism of the Holy Spirit is an experience necessary for the Christian if he is to become truly like Jesus in life and ministry. Through Holy Spirit baptism, Jesus lives most fully in the believer. As a result of this intimate connection with Jesus, the believer will begin to experience his greatest victories over sin and will develop the most meaningful relationship possible with his Savior.

The relationship between the baptism of the Holy Spirit and genuine Christian fellowship is also essential for the Christian to understand and experience. Even though we may receive the baptism of the Holy Spirit, we will not grow spiritually as God intends without a meaningful, mutually dependent fellowship with other Spirit-filled believers. To become Spirit filled, and remain somewhat isolated and independent of other Spirit-filled Christians, will not only hinder our spiritual growth but may lead to the loss of the fullness of the Spirit's presence in our life.

Bible-focused denominations, including Seventh-day Adventists, tend to be very intellectual in their religion. We know many vital truths of the Bible. Our evangelistic efforts focus on those truths that set us apart from other denominations. Hence, many who choose to become church members do so because of those truths.

One fact that has often troubled me is the general weakness of Seventh-day Adventists in the area of Christian fellowship. We are a rather independent group of believers. One has to have somewhat of an independent spirit to become a Seventh-day Adventist in the first place, for choosing to keep the seventh-day Sabbath sets us apart from the majority of other Christians.

I have often read the description of the believers following Pentecost:

"And they continued steadfastly in the apostles' doctrine and fellowship, and in breaking of bread, and in prayers" (Acts 2:42).

I knew we were "right on," as a church, when it came to doctrine. However, when it came to fellowship we didn't fare so well. I have observed that most Adventists are hard workers who provide for their families and do their best to attend the Sabbath morning worship service. Most church services are somewhat formal, with little or no time for interaction between believers. Hence, the average fellowship consists of warm greetings before and after church. Then most make their way home to return the next Sabbath. Many of our churches have a midweek prayer meeting, which usually consists of a biblical presentation by the pastor and a season of prayer. However, most of our church members feel they are too busy or too tired to attend this midweek service.

The average fellowship consists of warm greetings before and after church.

I have often felt that as Seventh-day Adventist Christians, fellowship should play a more important role than it does. The next seven devotionals will show why Spirit-filled Christians must enter into close fellowship with others who are Spirit filled if they want to grow into the fullness of Christ and be ready for His return.

Personal Reflection and Discussion

What are the characteristics of the early Christian church, as listed in Acts 2:42?

____

____

Reflect on how much genuine Christian fellowship you are now having, or have had in the past.

____

____

Why do you think Christian fellowship is important in one's life today? ______________

____

____

Why do you think Christian fellowship is necessary to be ready for Christ's second coming?

____

____

Prayer Activity

Call your prayer partner and discuss this devotional with him/her.
Pray with your prayer partner:

- **for God to continue to baptize each of you with His Holy Spirit.**
- **for God to bring revival into your life and His church.**
- **for God to open your understanding as to why Christian fellowship is important.**
- **for the individuals on your prayer list.**

INCLUDE THE FOLLOWING BIBLE VERSE IN YOUR PRAYER:
"'For a brief moment I abandoned you, but with deep compassion I will bring you back. In a surge of anger I hid my face from you for a moment, but with everlasting kindness I will have compassion on you,' says the Lord your Redeemer. . . . 'Though the mountains be shaken and the hills be removed, yet my unfailing love for you will not be shaken nor my covenant of peace be removed,' says the Lord, who has compassion on you" (Isa. 54:7-10, NIV).

Don't abandon us to our sin—have compassion on us
and deliver us from our sinfulness.
Restore us to spiritual strength.

Day 34

The Early Church and Fellowship

I personally believe the Lord is moving upon His people to look more closely at what the New Testament church was like. Seventh-day Adventists have viewed themselves as God's remnant for many years. We have sought to hold true to the teachings of God's Word, as did the New Testament church. I believe that now the Lord is calling us to not only continue "steadfastly in the apostles' doctrine," but to continue steadfastly in "fellowship, and in breaking of bread, and in prayers" (Acts 2:42). God is calling His children to be His remnant people just like the New Testament early church, not only in doctrine but in fellowship, as well. Fellowship is an important aspect to being God's remnant people. With this in mind, let's take a closer look at what God's early church was like.

The book of Acts tells us that the early Christians met both in the temple and from house to house:

"And they, continuing daily with one accord in the temple, and breaking bread from house to house, did eat their meat with gladness and singleness of heart" (verse 46).

As the Christians became unwelcome in the Jewish temples, their homes became the focal point of their worship and fellowship. The homes of the believers were the places where they met for praise, fellowship and teaching. Many verses mention the homes in the New Testament where the Christians met:

"And when they were come in, they went up into an upper room, where abode both Peter, and James, and John, and Andrew, Philip, and Thomas, Bartholomew, and Matthew, James the son of Alphaeus, and Simon Zelotes, and Judas the brother of James" (Acts 1:13).

"And a certain woman named Lydia, a seller of purple, of the city of Thyatira, which worshipped God, heard us: whose heart the Lord opened, that she attended unto the things which were spoken of Paul. And when she was baptized, and her household, she besought us, saying, If ye have judged me to be faithful to the Lord, come into my house, and abide there. And she constrained us" (Acts 16:14, 15).

"But the Jews which believed not, moved with envy, took unto them certain lewd fellows of the baser sort, and gathered a company, and set all the city on an uproar, and assaulted the house of Jason, and sought to bring them out to the people. And when they found them not, they drew Jason and certain brethren unto the rulers of the city, crying, These that have turned the world upside down are come hither also; Whom Jason hath received: and these all do contrary to the decrees of Caesar, saying that there is another king, one Jesus. And they troubled the people and the rulers of the city, when they heard these things. And when they had taken security of Jason, and of the other, they let them go" (Acts 17:5-9).

"And how I kept back nothing that was profitable unto you, but have shewed you, and have taught you publicly, and from house to house" (Acts 20:20).

"Likewise greet the church that is in their house. Salute my wellbeloved Epaenetus, who is the firstfruits of Achaia unto Christ" (Rom. 16:5).

"And I baptized also the household of Stephanas: besides, I know not whether I baptized any other" (1 Cor. 1:16). "The churches of Asia salute you. Aquila and Priscilla salute you much in the Lord, with the church that is in their house" (1 Cor. 16:19).

"Salute the brethren which are in Laodicea, and Nymphas, and the church which is in his house" (Col. 4:15).

The apostles certainly understood the importance of a small home fellowship. For three and one half years they had worshipped and fellowshipped with Jesus in this manner. We can understand how natural it was for the apostles to continue this type of small group fellowship as hundreds and thousands of individuals accepted Christ. The home fellowship style of church would make it much easier to assimilate and organize the large numbers joining the church even on a daily basis:

"Praising God, and having favour with all the people. And the Lord added to the church daily such as should be saved" (Acts 2:47).

These small fellowship groups served the growth of the church well. It is estimated that by the third century, six million Christians lived in the Roman Empire. These small fellowship groups were conducive to growth. New members were assimilated quickly and thoroughly. It would also be evident that these groups were not just to nurture but were evangelistic in nature. The home groups enabled the church to grow even in times of severe persecution. Also, as the numbers of a home church grew, participants would be forced to divide and form a new group in another home.

The close, intimate fellowship that results from the smaller group creates a very close bond between members of the group. Mutual encouragement more readily takes place. It is in this kind of setting that fellow believers receive strength from one another. Humankind is created to stand stronger when united with others than when alone. Christians today need the strength that comes from the close, intimate fellowship the early church experienced. As God said in the beginning, "it is not good for the man to be alone" (Gen. 2:18, NIV). It is not good for the Christian to try to withstand the forces of Satan and the world alone.

Personal Reflection and Discussion

Where did the early Christians meet for fellowship, and why?

____

What are the benefits of home fellowship groups?

____

Why do you think Christian fellowship is important in one's life today?

____

____

Do you think there will be a time when home fellowship will become necessary? Why, or why not?

____

____

Would you like to be a part of a Spirit-filled home fellowship group? If yes, how can you become part of one?

____

____

Prayer Activity

Call your prayer partner and discuss this devotional with him/her.
Pray with your prayer partner:

- **for God to continue to baptize each of you with His Holy Spirit.**
- **for God to bring revival into your life and His church.**
- **for God to lead you to become part of a fellowship group.**
- **for the individuals on your prayer list.**

INCLUDE THE FOLLOWING BIBLE VERSE IN YOUR PRAYER:
"As the bridegroom rejoiceth over the bride, so shall thy God rejoice over thee. I have set watchmen upon thy walls, O Jerusalem, which shall never hold their peace day nor night: ye that make mention of the Lord, keep not silence, and give him no rest, till he establish, and till he make Jerusalem a praise in the earth" (Isa. 62:5-7).

Cause us to pray to You constantly
until You revive us and make us a praise to Your name in this community.

Day 35

Spirit Baptism and Fellowship Groups

The baptism of the Holy Spirit and fellowship groups go hand in hand. Both are necessary for the Christian to grow into the fullness of Christ. The baptism of the Holy Spirit is essential for the core members of a fellowship group in order for the group to function as God intends. We see this clearly illustrated in the experience of Christ and the disciples. The 12 disciples were in a very close personal, group relationship with Christ and one another for three-and-a-half years. Yet we find them bickering among themselves on the way to the Passover supper just before Christ was to be taken by the mob and ultimately crucified:

"And there was also a strife among them, which of them should be accounted the greatest" (Luke 22:24).

They had not yet attained the level of loving, committed fellowship with God or each other during those years. Simply being a part of a fellowship group, of which Christ was the leader, was not enough to bring about the changes necessary for them to grow up into the fullness of Christ. Later, we find that they were changed dramatically. What made the difference? Their receiving the baptism of the Holy Spirit on the day of Pentecost made the difference. From that day forward they, and all others who were present, entered into the genuine Christian fellowship that God desires every believer to experience:

"And they continued steadfastly in the apostles' doctrine and fellowship, and in breaking of bread, and in prayers." "And they, continuing daily with one accord in the temple, and breaking bread from house to house, did eat their meat with gladness and singleness of heart, praising God, and having favour with all the people. And the Lord added to the church daily such as should be saved" (Acts 2:42, 46, 47).

The early church's fellowship way of doing church cannot happen during the traditional Sabbath morning worship service because of the interrelational dynamics required between Spirit-filled believers. The only way this kind of fellowship experience can happen is in small Christian fellowship groups. The traditional Sabbath worship service is important. The point is that alone is not enough.

The importance of Spirit-filled believers fellowshipping together in small groups is demonstrated by two illustrations. Paul gives us one illustration of the necessity of a continued living connection between believers in his first letter to the Corinthians, chapter 12. He uses the analogy of the human body to describe the church and its members. He points out how necessary it is for each body part to minister to the body. Spirit-filled believers need one another. They are to minister to one another just as your heart, right hand, eyes, etc., minister to the other parts of your body. From this analogy it is evident that it is necessary for each body part to remain in close, living connection with the other body parts. It is the home fellowship groups that enable the Spirit-baptized believer to keep a close, living connection with the body of Christ, which enables members of the body to minister to one another:

"But the manifestation of the Spirit is given to every man to profit withal. For to one is given by the Spirit the word of wisdom; to another the word of knowledge by the same Spirit; to another faith by the same Spirit; to another the gifts of healing by the same Spirit; to another the working of miracles; to another prophecy; to another discerning of spirits; to another divers kinds of tongues; to another the interpretation of tongues: but all these worketh that one and the selfsame Spirit, dividing to every man severally as he will. For as the body is one, and hath many members, and all the members of that one body, being many, are one body: so also is Christ" (1 Cor. 12:7-12).

"And he gave some, apostles; and some, prophets; and some, evangelists; and some, pastors and teachers; for the perfecting of the saints, for the work of the ministry, for the edifying of the body of Christ: till we all come in the unity of the faith, and of the knowledge of the Son of God, unto a perfect man, unto the measure of the stature of the fulness of Christ: That we henceforth be no more children, tossed to and fro, and carried about with every wind of doctrine, by the sleight of men, and cunning craftiness, whereby they lie in wait to deceive; But speaking the truth in love, may grow up into him in all things, which is the head, even Christ: from whom the whole body fitly joined together and compacted by that which every joint supplieth, according to the effectual working in the measure of every part, maketh increase of the body unto the edifying of itself in love" (Eph. 4:11-16).

Another illustration of the importance of home fellowship groups can be seen around any campfire. Think for a moment of a time when you were sitting around a camp fire and watching the embers burn. In order to keep the fire going it was important that you kept the embers close together and occasionally put on new wood. If a burning ember became separated from the other burning embers it would soon lose its fire and go out. This clearly illustrates the importance of close Christian fellowship. In order for the Spirit-baptized believer to keep the "fire" from going out in his life, he needs not only to continually ask God for the Spirit's infilling (Eph. 5:18), but he must also continually keep in fellowship with other Spirit-filled believers.

Personal Reflection and Discussion

What is the relationship between the baptism of the Holy Spirit and Christian fellowship groups?

Was the disciples' association with Jesus for three-and-a-half years enough to prepare them for the close fellowship Jesus wanted them to have? Why, or why not?

What illustration did the apostle Paul use to indicate how closely Christians should be associated with one another?

What illustration from nature also teaches this lesson?

Do you feel close, Christian fellowship is important for your spiritual life? Why?

Prayer Activity

Call your prayer partner and discuss this devotional with him/her.
Pray with your prayer partner:

- **for God to continue to baptize each of you with His Holy Spirit.**
- **for God to bring revival into your life and His church.**
- **for God to bless your efforts to become part of a fellowship group.**
- **for the individuals on your prayer list.**

INCLUDE THE FOLLOWING BIBLE VERSE IN YOUR PRAYER:
"My soul is weary with sorrow; strengthen me according to your word" (Ps. 119:28, NIV).

My sinful condition has weakened me.
Turn me from my sin.
Strengthen me spiritually as You have promised.

Day 36

The Church

The Greek word used in the New Testament for church is *ekklesia,* which means "called-out ones." When men and women respond to the Holy Spirit's conviction to accept Christ as their Savior, they become part of *ekklesia,* the called-out ones.

When we study the New Testament we discover that there are two very important aspects of church. Those who are called out are called to believe the teachings of the Bible. Paul describes the church with these words:

"But if I tarry long, that thou mayest know how thou oughtest to behave thyself in the house of God, which is the church of the living God, the pillar and ground of the truth" (1 Tim. 3:15).

Paul calls the church the "pillar and ground of the truth." Those called out are to believe, live, and teach the truths of God's word.

There is another important aspect of church revealed in John's first letter:

"That which we have seen and heard declare we unto you, that ye also may have fellowship with us: and truly our fellowship is with the Father, and with his Son Jesus Christ" (1 John 1:3).

This second vital aspect of church is what the New Testament calls "fellowship." In the simplest sense, fellowship is certainly not a new concept. In fact, in one sense we fellowship when we worship at church on Sabbath or when we attend a church social together. However, the New Testament concept of fellowship is much broader than most Christians realize.

The Greek word translated fellowship is *koinonia.* The noun form of this term means to share in, participate in, or to be actively involved in. The verb form means to communicate, distribute, and impart. Hence, to *koinonia* together means much more than simply sitting together in the sanctuary for Sabbath worship or playing games together at a social. The New Testament meaning of fellowship goes much deeper. In essence, it means ministering to one another. It is not simply knowing one another's names, knowing where we live, and warmly greeting one another at church Sabbath morning. It means sharing one another's hopes, dreams, struggles, and pains. It means allowing God to use us to minister to one another. According to the New Testament, a church fellowship is an assembly of individuals, called out of the world by God to become a community, with common biblical beliefs and who actively communicate, distribute, impart, and minister to one another.

> ***Fellowship means sharing one another's hopes, dreams, struggles and pains. It means allowing God to use us to minister to one another.***

If Christians are not in that kind of relationship with one another, they are falling far short of God's plan for His church. We may be keeping the Sabbath and going to church, but if we are not in genuine *koinonia* Christian fellowship, we are not actually experiencing God's definition of church to the fullest extent.

Personal Reflection and Discussion

What does the word *church* mean in the New Testament?

____

What are two aspects of the Christian church in the New Testament?

____

____

What does it mean to be in *koinonia* fellowship with one another?

____

____

Are you involved in *koinonia* fellowship with any Christians?

____

If yes, what has been your experience with this kind of fellowship?

____

If no, would you like to be in this kind of fellowship?

____

Prayer Activity

Call your prayer partner and discuss this devotional with him/her.
Pray with your prayer partner:

- **for God to continue to baptize each of you with His Holy Spirit.**
- **for God to bring revival into your life and His church.**
- **for God to bless your efforts to become part of a *koinonia* fellowship group, or to bless your fellowship group if you are in one.**
- **for the individuals on your prayer list.**

INCLUDE THE FOLLOWING BIBLE VERSE IN YOUR PRAYER:
"O fear the Lord, ye his saints: for there is no want to them that fear him" (Ps. 34:9).

Cause us to fear and reverence You with all our hearts.
Deliver us from the things that keep us from
having what we need spiritually.

Day 37

The Family of God

Sin broke apart the family of God. The plan of redemption was established to restore this family. Paul addresses those who have responded to God's call in their lives in the following way:

"Now therefore ye are no more strangers and foreigners, but fellowcitizens with the saints, and of the household of God" (Eph. 2:19).

The Greek word translated "household" is *oikeios.* When we become a believer in Jesus Christ we become a member of God's household. We become a member of His family.

Traditionally, we tend to think of church in a larger sense, the corporate or congregational aspect. We do not tend to think of church in terms of a smaller family. However, the early church from the biblical and historical perspective was made up of small home fellowships. These fellowship groups functioned as family.

When Paul describes his own feelings toward the Thessalonian family of God, he expresses the relationship that is to be experienced in the family of God:

"We loved you so much that we were delighted to share with you not only the gospel of God but our lives as well, because you had become so dear to us" (1 Thess. 2:8, NIV).

These kinds of endearing relationships cannot happen in the larger congregational setting. If our church activities consist primarily of coming to church on Sabbath morning, greeting our friends, and then returning home, we cannot possibly achieve this level of family relationship.

For example, what if you heard about a family that remained separated from one another during the week and then came together once a week for an hour or two, briefly greeted one another, then sat in rows, and heard someone give a lecture. Afterward, they went their separate ways until seven days later when they associated "together" by again greeting one another, sitting in rows, and listening to another lecture. What would you think about that family's togetherness? I think you would question if they were really a family. Most would certainly conclude that their style of family togetherness had much room for improvement. Amazingly and yet sadly, most Christians seek to be a church family using this pattern of family.

In a healthy family the members know each other intimately. They know one another's fears, hopes, dreams, frustrations, and struggles. In a loving, caring family the members are there to encourage one another with words and actions.

The family of God is to function in the same way. However, God's family has one significant advantage over the average family in the world. God's family experiences the fruit and gifts of the Spirit functioning in their midst. God Himself is the One ministering to the family members. He does this through each member of the family as they continue to receive the baptism of the Holy Spirit. The intimate relationship with God this daily baptism brings allows Christ to live in and minister through each believer, but this dynamic of family can only take place in the smaller fellowship group setting.

In a loving family the members are there to encourage one another with words and actions.

Personal Reflection and Discussion

What kind of relationship did God originally plan for His children?

What did sin do to God's plan?

What does the plan of redemption do for God's broken family?

What kind of relationships does God intend His church members to have with one another?

What setting is most conducive for this to happen?

Would you like to experience God's ideal for His church family?

Prayer Activity

Call your prayer partner and discuss this devotional with him/her.

Pray with your prayer partner:

- **for God to continue to baptize each of you with His Holy Spirit.**
- **for God to bring revival into your life and His church.**
- **for God to lead you into the kind of church family experience He desires you to have.**
- **for the individuals on your prayer list.**

INCLUDE THE FOLLOWING BIBLE VERSE IN YOUR PRAYER:
"Many are the afflictions of the righteous: but the Lord delivereth him out of them all" (Ps. 34:19).

Lead us to be Your righteous people who have turned from their sinful ways. Deliver us from every affliction Satan tries to bring on us.

Day 38

The Fruit of the Spirit and Fellowship

Two essential elements of effective Christian fellowship groups are the fruits and gifts of the Spirit manifested in the lives of the participants. There is only one way these can be present: the participants must be Spirit filled.

In today's devotional we will consider the role the fruits of the Spirit play in fellowship. If the fruits of the Spirit are not present and maturing in the participants' lives, they will not receive the full benefit of the fellowship group. Neither will they have the character necessary to minister to their fellow participants. The fruits of the Spirit are listed in Paul's letter to the Galatians:

"But the fruit of the Spirit is love, joy, peace, longsuffering, gentleness, goodness, faith, meekness, temperance: against such there is no law" (Gal. 5:22, 23).

The first fruit is love. The Greek word here is *agape* love, the highest form of love. It is the kind of love with which God loves us, doing what is best for the one loved. Jesus described this kind of love in Matthew 5:44:

"But I say unto you, Love your enemies, bless them that curse you, do good to them that hate you, and pray for them which despitefully use you, and persecute you."

Paul described *agape* love in 1 Corinthians 13:4-7:

"Charity suffereth long, and is kind; charity envieth not; charity vaunteth not itself, is not puffed up, doth not behave itself unseemly, seeketh not her own, is not easily provoked, thinketh no evil; rejoiceth not in iniquity, but rejoiceth in the truth; beareth all things, believeth all things, hopeth all things, endureth all things."

This fruit of love will allow the participant of a fellowship group to manifest understanding and sensitivity to others in the group. His/her example will tend to quiet any harsh tones or attitudes in others. Also, he/she will not have a judgmental attitude when a participant shares with the group his personal struggles. Rather, the fruit of love will cause him/her to feel empathy and compassion. He/she will reach out with healing, encouraging, redemptive words to the one hurting.

Every fruit that follows in Paul's list plays a similarly significant role in maintaining the kind of atmosphere that is necessary for the Christian fellowship group to function as God intends.

These qualities, which comprise the fruits of the Spirit, are impossible to achieve apart from the infilling of the Spirit. Spirit-filled Christians are necessary if the fellowship group is to fulfill its purpose of providing an atmosphere in which all participants can grow into the fullness of Christ:

"And he gave some, apostles; and some, prophets; and some, evangelists; and some, pastors and teachers; for the perfecting of the saints, for the work of the ministry, for the edifying of the body of Christ: till we all come in the unity of the faith, and of the knowledge of the Son of God, unto a perfect man, unto the measure of the stature of the fulness of Christ: that we henceforth be no more children, tossed to and fro, and carried about with every wind of doctrine, by the sleight of men, and cunning craftiness, whereby they lie in wait to deceive; But speaking the truth in love, may grow up into him in all things, which is the head, even Christ: from whom the whole body fitly joined together and compacted by that which every joint supplieth, according to the effectual working in the measure of every part, maketh increase of the body unto the edifying of itself in love" (Eph. 4:11-16).

The fruits of the Spirit, which are only manifest in

the life of the believer by the baptism of the Holy Spirit, must be present in the lives of the core members of the fellowship group. These fruits bring the character of Christ into the group. It is through people that God loves us. So it will be through the Spirit-filled Christians that God will reveal His love to all who come to the fellowship, whether they are Christian or nonchristian.

Personal Reflection and Discussion

What must each fellowship participant have in order for the fruits of the Spirit to be present?

____

List the fruits of the Spirit and describe how each one is a blessing to those in the fellowship group.

____

____

____

____

____

____

____

How do you plan to become a part of this kind of fellowship group?

____

Prayer Activity

Call your prayer partner and discuss this devotional with him/her.

Pray with your prayer partner:

- **for God to continue to baptize each of you with His Holy Spirit.**
- **for God to bring revival into your life and His church.**
- **for God to manifest the fruits of the Spirit in your life and to lead you to a Spirit-filled fellowship group.**
- **for the individuals on your prayer list.**

INCLUDE THE FOLLOWING BIBLE VERSE IN YOUR PRAYER:
"You will go out in joy and be led forth in peace; the mountains and hills will burst into song before you, and all the trees of the field will clap their hands. Instead of the thornbush will grow the pine tree, and instead of briers the myrtle will grow. This will be for the Lord's renown, for an everlasting sign which will not be destroyed" (Isa. 55:12, 13, NIV).

Restore us to fullness of joy and peace in You.
Remove the spiritual thorn bushes and briers that are in our lives and congregation.
May there be great joy and rejoicing in You.
Glorify Your name in this congregation.

Day 39

The Gifts of the Spirit and Fellowship

Another essential ingredient for a fellowship group to be successful is the functioning of the gifts of the Spirit in the group. Since spiritual gifts are manifested through Spirit-filled believers, it is essential that the participants be baptized in the Holy Spirit.

Several chapters in the New Testament discuss spiritual gifts. The most prominent scriptures concerning spiritual gifts are found in Paul's letters:

"For as we have many members in one body, and all members have not the same office: So we, being many, are one body in Christ, and every one members one of another. Having then gifts differing according to the grace that is given to us, whether prophecy, let us prophesy according to the proportion of faith; or ministry, let us wait on our ministering: or he that teacheth, on teaching; or he that exhorteth, on exhortation: he that giveth, let him do it with simplicity; he that ruleth, with diligence; he that sheweth mercy, with cheerfulness" (Rom. 12:4-8).

"But the manifestation of the Spirit is given to every man to profit withal. For to one is given by the Spirit the word of wisdom; to another the word of knowledge by the same Spirit; to another faith by the same Spirit; to another the gifts of healing by the same Spirit; to another the working of miracles; to another prophecy; to another discerning of spirits; to another divers kinds of tongues; to another the interpretation of tongues: but all these worketh that one and the selfsame Spirit, dividing to every man severally as he will. For as the body is one, and hath many members, and all the members of that one body, being many, are one body: so also is Christ" (1 Cor. 12:7-12).

"But unto every one of us is given grace according to the measure of the gift of Christ. Wherefore he saith, When he ascended up on high, he led captivity captive, and gave gifts unto men. . . . And he gave some, apostles; and some, prophets; and some, evangelists; and some, pastors and teachers" (Eph. 4:7-11).

These gifts serve a most important role in the spiritual growth of the individual believer and the church. Paul uses the analogy of the human body and lists various body parts, pointing out the importance each part plays in the functioning of the whole body. The conclusion is clear. It is necessary that every body part function effectively in order for the body as a whole to be healthy and effective in fulfilling its mission:

"For the body is not one member, but many. If the foot shall say, Because I am not the hand, I am not of the body; is it therefore not of the body? And if the ear shall say, Because I am not the eye, I am not of the body; is it therefore not of the body? If the whole body were an eye, where were the hearing? If the whole were hearing, where were the smelling? But now hath God set the members every one of them in the body, as it hath pleased him. And if they were all one member, where were the body? But now are they many members, yet but one body. And the eye cannot say unto the hand, I have no need of thee: nor again the head to the feet, I have no need of you. Nay, much more those members of the body, which seem to be more feeble, are necessary" (1 Cor. 12:14-22).

Paul states that "the members should have the same care one for another (verse 25). When functioning in the church body, the gifts prove a great blessing to each member of the body of Christ.

It should be very clear from Paul's description that

the gifts of the Spirit are necessary if the individual Christian and church are to grow. Paul's statement that members should have the "same care one for another" is a clear reference to genuine Christian fellowship. In order to experience a deep empathy for our fellow members we must truly know them. We must be free to share our deepest needs, struggles, hopes, and dreams if we are to minister to one another. Paul was referring to the importance of ministering to one another when he wrote:

"Bear ye one another's burdens, and so fulfill the law of Christ" (Gal. 6:2).

This kind of fellowship cannot happen by doing church in the traditional way. If our only connection with the members of our church is meeting them on Sabbath morning and giving them a warm greeting, it will be impossible for biblical fellowship to happen.

The gifts of the Spirit will function in a very practical manner in blessing those in fellowship. For example, the gift of teacher in the New Testament is one who instructs in God's Word. It is readily understood how vital it is to have this gift in a fellowship group. The group's goal is not to become primarily a study group. There is a place for intensive Bible study; however, the main focus of a Christian fellowship group is worship and healing fellowship. The gift of teaching that fits into this purpose will be a great blessing to all who attend. The lessons will be generally short ones from Scripture rather than a long teaching session. The emphasis will be placed on the practical application of Scripture to the individual issues that arise in the group setting.

Another example is the gift of exhortation. When this gift is present, God will use it to speak words of encouragement, comfort, and hope, especially to group participants who are hurting and dealing with some serious issue in their lives. The manifestation of this gift brings practical, uplifting biblical counsel to the group members. Such spiritual gifts being manifested in a Christian fellowship group will enable the Spirit to minister to all participants.

Personal Reflection and Discussion

What must each fellowship participant have so that the gifts of the Spirit are present?

____

List several gifts of the Spirit and describe how each one will be used by God to minister to those in the fellowship group.

____

____

____

____

Have you seen God manifest spiritual gifts through you to minister to others? If yes, which gifts?

____

____

Prayer Activity

Call your prayer partner and discuss this devotional with him/her.
Pray with your prayer partner:

- **for God to continue to baptize each of you with His Holy Spirit.**
- **for God to bring revival into your life and His church.**
- **for God to manifest the gifts of the Spirit in your life that He has chosen for you, and to use you to minister to others through these gifts.**
- **for the individuals on your prayer list.**

INCLUDE THE FOLLOWING BIBLE VERSE IN YOUR PRAYER:
"Blow the trumpet in Zion, sanctify a fast, call a solemn assembly: gather the people, sanctify the congregation, assemble the elders, gather the children . . . Let the priests, the ministers of the Lord, weep between the porch and the altar, and let them say, Spare thy people, O Lord, and give not thine heritage to reproach, that the heathen should rule over them: wherefore should they say among the people, Where is their God? Then will the Lord be jealous for his land, and pity his people. Yea, the Lord will answer and say unto his people, Behold, I will send you corn, and wine, and oil, and ye shall be satisfied therewith: and I will no more make you a reproach among the heathen" (Joel 2:15-19).

Give us a strong desire to solemnly gather together and seek You earnestly in prayer.
Glorify Your name through us that others will see that You are with us.
Have mercy and pity on us and revive us in every way
that we will flourish and prosper as Your people.

Day 40

Fellowship Groups and Church Growth

The fellowship of believers will play an important role in their spiritual, emotional, and even physical restoration that God wants each one of us to experience.

Growth should—and must be—the goal of every Christian fellowship group. If the group is not growing, it is not functioning in the manner God intends. Remember, the baptism of the Holy Spirit is given for both our personal spiritual growth and for the spreading of the gospel:

"But ye shall receive power, after that the Holy Ghost is come upon you: and ye shall be witnesses unto me both in Jerusalem, and in all Judaea, and in Samaria, and unto the uttermost part of the earth" (Acts 1:8).

Hence, nonbelievers, or individuals who are not church members, should be present.

It is essential for our own personal spiritual growth to be involved in winning others to Christ. We must personally heed God's command to be "fruitful, and multiply" (Gen. 1:28). God could have used angels for the work of soul winning; however, He did not. Why? He knows the importance of each of us being personally involved in reaching others for Christ. Ellen White makes a significant statement concerning this:

"If you will go to work as Christ designs that His disciples shall, and win souls for Him, you will feel the need of a deeper experience and a greater knowledge in divine things, and will hunger and thirst after righteousness. You will plead with God, and your faith will be strengthened and your soul will drink deeper drafts at the well of salvation. Encountering opposition and trials will drive you to the Bible and prayer. You will grow in grace and the knowledge of Christ, and will develop a rich experience" (*Steps to Christ,* p. 80).

The support the fellowship group gives will play a significant role in our efforts to reach out to others. The members of the group will join in prayer for those we are reaching out to. The counsel of those more experienced in soul winning will be a great benefit to us. The spiritual fathers and mothers in the group will be used by God to assist the less experienced in leading others to Christ.

The fellowship group will provide a marvelous environment for the one seeking God, for he will find loving, caring individuals who will accept him as he is. The seeker will find himself in an environment in which God's Spirit can work in a powerful way for his conversion to Christ. We read in the book of Acts that as the early Christians continued to fellowship together the church grew:

"And they, continuing daily with one accord in the temple, and breaking bread from house to house, did eat their meat with gladness and singleness of heart, praising God, and having favour with all the people. And the Lord added to the church daily such as should be saved" (Acts 2:46, 47).

God will minister to both the believers and nonbelievers who are present in the fellowship group. He will do this by means of the fruits and gifts of the Spirit. The small fellowship group setting completely changes the traditional impersonal dynamic of evangelism when individuals attend an evangelistic meeting in response to a mailed advertisement. The very essence of the fellowship group is close, intimate, interpersonal relationships. When a nonbeliever comes to experience Christianity and new biblical truths in the setting of this fellowship, he does so in the context of a close interpersonal relationship with a member of the group. He is placed in a redemptive environment that is conducive to his personal spiritual growth.

Personal Reflection and Discussion

What are the two purposes of genuine Christian fellowship groups?

____

List suggestions on how a fellowship group can become effective in reaching others outside the group for Christ?

____

____

____

____

____

How do you plan to become part of a growing fellowship group and be used by God to share Christ with others?

____

Prayer Activity

Call your prayer partner and discuss this devotional with him/her.
Pray with your prayer partner:

- **for God to continue to baptize each of you with His Holy Spirit.**
- **for God to bring revival into your life and His church.**
- **for God to lead you to become part of a growing fellowship group and be used by Him to bring others to Christ.**
- **for the individuals on your prayer list.**

INCLUDE THE FOLLOWING BIBLE VERSE IN YOUR PRAYER:
"Be glad then, ye children of Zion, and rejoice in the Lord your God. . . and he will cause to come down for you the rain, the former rain, and the latter rain. . . And ye shall eat in plenty, and be satisfied, and praise the name of the Lord your God, that hath dealt wondrously. . . I will pour out my spirit upon all flesh; and your sons and your daughters shall prophesy, your old men shall dream dreams, your young men shall see visions" (Joel 2:23-28).

Give us an earnest desire for Your Holy Spirit
lead us to pray for the early rain baptism of the Holy Spirit in our lives
and for the latter rain outpouring of Your Holy Spirit.
Manifest the gifts of Your Spirit through us and use us to glorify Your name.
Reveal Your power in our midst and in our community
that many will come to know You as their God and Savior.

Appendix A: *Daily Prayer List*

List five or more individuals who have either left the church, or were never members of the church, that you plan to pray for and reach out to during the next 40 days in order for the Lord to bring them into His fold in preparation for Christ's soon return. (They should be individuals living in your area in order to invite them to church sometime during the next 40 days.)

____

____

____

____

____

Pray for these individuals every day claiming the scriptures below on their behalf. These are taken from the *Praying Church Source Book,* pages 128-129.

- That God will draw them to Himself (John 6:44)
- That they seek to know God (Acts 17:27)
- That they believe the Word of God (1 Thess. 2:13)
- That Satan is bound from blinding them to the truth and that his influences in their life be "cast down" (2 Cor. 4:4; 10:4, 5)
- That the Holy Spirit works in them (John 16:8-13)
- That they turn from sin (Acts 3:19)
- That they believe in Christ as Savior (John 1:12)
- That they obey Christ as Lord (Matt. 7:21)
- That they take root and grow in Christ (Col. 2:6, 7)

Prayerfully use the *Activities to Show You Care* (see Appendix B) list to determine what the Lord wants you to do to reach out to those on your prayer list during the next 40 days.

Appendix B: *Activities to Show You Care*

The following are suggestions of things you can do for those on your prayer list to show that you care for them. Add to this list as the Lord leads.

1. Call to say what you appreciate about them
2. Mail a card sharing what God puts in your heart to tell them
3. Send a piece of encouraging literature
4. Call and pray with them
5. Give an invitation to visit you in your home for a meal
6. Give an invitation to go out to lunch with you
7. Send a birthday card
8. Send a card expressing encouragement
9. Take something you cooked
10. Invite to accompany you shopping, trip to museum, etc.
11. Send a get well, or sympathy card when needed
12. Give their child a birthday card and gift when appropriate
13. Invite them to attend church with you
14. At the appropriate time ask if he/she would like to receive Bible studies.
15. ______________________________
16. ______________________________
17. ______________________________
18. ______________________________
19. ______________________________
20. ______________________________

Appendix C: *Suggested Greeting for Prayer Contact*

Hello, ________________________________ (*interest's name*).

This is ____________________________________ (*your name*).

My church is having a special emphasis on prayer, and is requesting that we choose five individuals to pray for during the next 40 days.

I have chosen you for one of my five to pray for.

What would you like for me to especially pray for in your behalf, such as family, job, a health issue, etc.?

(*Write down what they want you to pray for* below).

____

I appreciate the opportunity to especially pray for this for you during the next 40 days.

Thanks, ___________________________ (*interest's name*). I'll keep in touch.

Appendix D:
After 40 Days of Prayer and Devotional Studies. . .

Now that you have completed the 40 days of prayer and devotional studies, you probably don't want the experience you are having with the Lord, and the fellowship you are enjoying to fade away. So, what should you do next?

One possibility is that you begin studying in greater detail the subjects presented in this devotional. Each section has been based on one of five books I have written. The titles of the books in the order of the devotional sections are:

- *The Baptism of the Holy Spirit*
- *Spirit Baptism and Prayer*
- *Spirit Baptism and Evangelism*
- *Spirit Baptism and Abiding in Christ*
- *Spirit Baptism and New Wineskin Fellowship*

If this is your desire, I would suggest you start with the first book listed, *The Baptism of the Holy Spirit,* and begin studying it with your prayer partner or fellowship group who participated in the 40 days of prayer and devotional study with you. You may want to invite others to join you and your group. Then individually and as a group continue to progress through each book. This will enable the Lord to strengthen the experience with Him that He has begun in your life during the past 40 days.

Or if you want to, move on to other subjects related to the baptism of the Holy Spirit. The following books that I have written could be used for individual and group study to learn about other aspects of the Spirit-baptized experience. They can be studied in any order as the Lord leads.

- *Spirit Baptism and Waiting on God*
- *Spirit Baptism and Christ's Glorious Return*
- *Spirit Baptism and Deliverance*
- *Spirit Baptism and the 1888 Message of Righteousness by Faith*
- *Spirit Baptism and Earth's Final Events*

Second, continue to pray for those on your prayer list and reach out to them. Also, add others to your list as the Lord leads, and as a group consider activities to plan to invite those on the prayer lists to attend.

Christ wants personal daily devotional study, prayer, and reaching out to others to become an integral part of every Christian's life. If this aspect of your life ends with the 40 days of prayer and devotional study you will not grow into the fullness of Christ that He desires you to experience. Also, this is the only way to be ready for Christ's soon return. For it is the only way our intimate relationship with Christ develops and grows. May the Lord abundantly bless your continued devotional study and prayer time with Him, and your efforts to share Him with others.

Note: All books listed are available through most Adventist Book Centers or at www.spiritbaptism.org.